ABOUT THE AUTHOR

Osho defies categorization. His thousands of talks cover everything from the individual quest for meaning to the most urgent social and political issues facing society today. Osho's books are not written but are transcribed from audio and video recordings of his extemporaneous talks to international audiences. As he puts it, 'So remember: whatever I am saying is not just for you ... I am talking also for the future generations.'

Osho has been described by the *Sunday Times* in London as one of the '1000 Makers of the 20th Century' and by American author Tom Robbins as 'the most dangerous man since Jesus Christ.' *Sunday Mid-Day* (India) has selected Osho as one of ten people – along with Gandhi, Nehru and Buddha – who have changed the destiny of India.

About his own work Osho has said that he is helping to create the conditions for the birth of a new kind of human being. He often characterizes this new human being as 'Zorba the Buddha' – capable both of enjoying the earthy pleasures of a Zorba the Greek and the silent serenity of a Gautama the Buddha.

Running like a thread through all aspects of Osho's talks and meditations is a vision that encompasses both the timeless wisdom of all ages past and the highest potential of today's (and tomorrow's) science and technology.

Osho is known for his revolutionary contribution to the science of inner transformation, with an approach to meditation that acknowledges the accelerated pace of contemporary life. His unique OSHO Active Meditations are designed to first release the accumulated stresses of body and mind, so that it is then easier to take an experience of stillness and thought-free relaxation into daily life.

OSHO
Living Dangerously
Ordinary Enlightenment for Extraordinary Times

WATKINS
Sharing Wisdom Since 1893

This edition first published in the UK and USA 2015 by Watkins,
an imprint of Watkins Media Limited,
Unit 11, Shepperton House,
89-93 Shepperton Road, London N1 3DF

enquiries@watkinspublishing.com

Text copyright © 2011, 2015 OSHO International Foundation
Design and typesetting © Watkins Media Limited 2011, 2015

English original: *Ordinary Enlightenment for Extraordiary Times,* by Osho

The material in this book is selected from various talks by Osho given to a
live audience. All of Osho's talks have been published in full as books, and
are also available as original audio recordings. Audio recordings and the
complete text archive can be found via the online OSHO Library at
www.osho.com

OSHO is a registered trademark of Osho International Foundation

www.osho.com/trademarks

10

Designed and typeset by Jerry Goldie Graphic Design
Printed and bound in the United Kingdom by TJ International Ltd.

A CIP record for this book is available from the British Library

ISBN: 978-1-78028-007-3

www.watkinspublishing.com

Contents

Preface

Total revolution has to arise from your very center.

That is my work here. I want every individual to clean the past from his mind completely. All his prejudices, all his thoughts – political, social, religious – everything has to be dropped. Just a clean slate, and you have arrived to the space of no-mind. No-mind is meditation, and no-mind is the revelation, and no-mind is the greatest rebellion that has ever happened.

In the past only very few people... a Gautam Buddha here and there, thousands of years pass and then comes one person who blossoms into a Buddha. But now there is no more time. You cannot postpone for tomorrow. Whatever you want to do has to be done now! For the first time, the present is becoming more and more important. Each day you are coming closer to choosing the alternative: either move towards becoming a Buddha or move towards becoming a corpse.

I don't think anybody wants to die, particularly when all life is at risk. The third world war cannot happen. We are going to prevent it!

I don't have any weapons, I don't have any nuclear missiles, but I have something greater and something far more effective. It is not to kill, it is to bring life to those who are living almost as if they are dead. It is bringing awareness to those who are behaving like somnambulists, walking in their sleep, talking in their sleep, not knowing exactly what they are doing and why they are doing it.

I want people to be so awake that their whole consciousness goes to the deepest part of their being, and also to the highest peak. A vertical growth – just like a tree grows. Its roots go down into the earth, and its branches spread towards the stars. Its blossoms flower into the sky, its nourishment comes from the deepest part of the earth. It is always balanced: the higher the tree goes, the deeper the roots. You cannot have a cedar of Lebanon tree, 400 or 500 years old, rising so high in the sky, with small roots. It will fall down immediately.

Life needs a balance between the depth and the height. I teach you both simultaneously. In your entering to the center in meditation, you are growing your roots deeper into the cosmos. And bringing the Buddha out from the hidden center is bringing your fragrance, bringing your grace, bringing your ecstasy higher, where it can blossom into the sky.

Your ecstasy is a movement towards the height and your

meditation is a movement towards the depth. And once you have both, your life becomes a celebration.

That is my work, to transform your life from a sad affair into a celebration.

Relax into your being, whoever you are. Don't impose any ideals. Don't drive yourself crazy; there is no need. Be – drop becoming. We are not going anywhere, we are just being here. And this moment is so beautiful, is such a benediction; don't bring any future into it, otherwise you will destroy it. Future is poisonous. Relax and enjoy. If I can help you to relax and enjoy, my work is done. If I can help you to drop your ideals, ideas about how you should be and how you should not be, if I can take away all the commandments that have been given to you, then my work is done. And when you are without any commandments, and when you live on the spur of the moment – natural, spontaneous, simple, ordinary – there is great celebration because you have arrived home.

My effort is to demolish all the rubbish that you have
collected down the ages.

If I can remove all that rubbish from your mind

and can give you a clean sky,

my work is done.

Without knowing, you will know.

The mystery, the mysterious, the poetry of life,

the music and the dance... all will become available
to you.

Introduction

Meditation:
The Master Key

Meditation opens the door of all the mysteries
of existence, of all the secrets of existence.
Meditation is the master key that opens all the
locks, and existence becomes an open book
for you.

What is meditation? Is it a technique that can be practiced?
Is it an effort that you have to do? Is it something that the
mind can achieve? It is not.

All that the mind can do cannot be meditation – it is
something beyond the mind, the mind is absolutely
helpless there. The mind cannot penetrate meditation;
where mind ends, meditation begins. This has to be
remembered, because in our life, whatsoever we do, we do

through the mind; whatsoever we achieve, we achieve through the mind. And then, when we turn inwards, we again start thinking in terms of techniques, methods, doings, because the whole of life's experience shows us that everything can be done by the mind. Yes. Except meditation, everything can be done by the mind; everything is done by the mind except meditation. Because meditation is not an achievement – it is already the case, it is your nature. It has not to be achieved; it has only to be recognized, it has only to be remembered. It is there waiting for you – just a turning in, and it is available. You have been carrying it always and always.

Meditation is your intrinsic nature – it is you, it is your being, it has nothing to do with your doings. You cannot have it, you cannot not have it, it cannot be possessed. It is not a thing. It is you. It is your being.

Once you understand what meditation is, things become very clear. Otherwise, you can go on groping in the dark.

Meditation is a state of clarity, not a state of mind. Mind is confusion. Mind is never clear. It cannot be. Thoughts create clouds around you – they are subtle clouds. A mist is created by them, and the clarity is lost. When thoughts disappear, when there are no more clouds around you, when you are in your simple beingness, clarity happens.

Then you can see far away; then you can see to the very end of existence; then your gaze becomes penetrating – to the very core of being.

Meditation is clarity, absolute clarity, of vision. You cannot think about it. You have to drop thinking. When I say, 'You have to drop thinking,' don't conclude in a hurry, because I have to use language. So I say, 'Drop thinking,' but if you start dropping, you will miss, because again you will reduce it to a doing.

'Drop thinking' simply means: don't do anything. Sit. Let thoughts settle themselves. Let mind drop on its own accord. You just sit gazing at the wall, in a silent corner, not doing anything at all. Relaxed, loose, with no effort. Not going anywhere. As if you are falling asleep awake – you are awake and you are relaxing, but the whole body is falling into sleep. You remain alert inside, but the whole body moves into deep relaxation.

Thoughts settle on their own accord, you need not jump amongst them, you need not try to put them right. It is as if a stream has become muddy...what do you do? Do you jump in it and start helping the stream to become clear? You will make it more muddy. You simply sit on the bank. You wait. There is nothing to be done. Because whatsoever you do will make the stream more muddy. If somebody has passed through a stream and the dead leaves have surfaced and the mud has arisen, just patience is needed. You simply sit on the bank. Watch, indifferently. And as the stream goes on flowing, the dead leaves will be taken away, and the mud will start settling because it cannot hang forever there. After a while, suddenly you will become aware – the stream is crystal-clear again.

Whenever a desire passes through your mind, the stream becomes muddy. So just sit. Don't try to do anything. In Japan, this 'just sitting' is called *zazen*; just sitting and doing nothing. And one day, meditation happens. Not that you bring it to you; it comes to you. And when it comes, you immediately recognize it; it has been always there but you were not looking in the right direction. The treasure has been with you but you were occupied somewhere else: in thoughts, in desires, in a thousand and one things. You were not interested in the only one thing... and that was your own being.

When energy turns in – what Buddha calls *parabvrutti*, the coming back of your energy to the source – suddenly clarity is attained. Then you can see clouds a thousand miles away, and you can hear ancient music in the pines. Then everything is available to you.

People are so cluttered with culture that first they have to be unburdened; that is a new need. Buddha never knew about it, so Buddhist methods are of no use right now. First you have to unburden yourself, then Buddhist methods can be used, otherwise not. And that is one of the problems that the West has to face. The East has exploded on the West. All the ancient methods and techniques are becoming available, and the people who are making them available are completely unaware about the modern mind. Those methods were developed 5,000 years before, some methods even 10,000 years before. Then there was a totally different kind of mind in the world, a very innocent, childlike mind. Those methods were perfectly in tune with that mind. Now man is no more a child, man has come of age, and the problems that naturally come with growth are there. Man is no more innocent.

Those methods were developed before Adam ate the fruit of the tree of knowledge. Modern man is full of apples; he is continuously eating from the tree of knowledge. He is so burdened, that unless he is defrosted those ancient methods cannot work. So humanistic psychology, psychoanalysis, psychosynthesis, and encounter, psychodrama and gestalt are of immense help; they are a basic need today. But they are incomplete, they only prepare the ground, they don't create the garden.

Man's pathology is there because man has to transcend. If you cannot transcend humanity, you will become pathological. All the psychological diseases are there because man has an inner capacity to go beyond humanity, to surpass humanity. And that energy is there – if you don't allow it, it will turn upon you, it will be destructive. All creative people are dangerous people, because if they are not allowed creativity, they will become destructive.

Man is the only animal on the earth who is creative; no other animal is so dangerous because no other animal creates. They simply live, they have a programmed life: they never go off the track. A dog lives like a dog and dies like a dog. He never tries to become a Buddha, and of course he never goes astray and becomes an Adolf Hitler. He simply follows the track. He is very conservative, orthodox, bourgeois; all animals except man are bourgeois. Man has something of the freak in him. He wants to do something, to go somewhere, to be; and if it is not allowed, if he cannot be a rose, then he would like to be a weed – but he would like to be something. If he cannot become a Buddha, he will become a criminal. If he cannot create poetry, he will create nightmares. If he cannot bloom, he will not allow anybody else to bloom.

So this is the work.

I have developed my own meditation techniques because I saw that for the modern man there are a few problems that are not covered in the old techniques. They were written perhaps 10,000 years ago for a totally different kind of mankind, a different kind of culture, a different kind of people. The modern man, the contemporary man, has some differences – over 10,000 years, it is absolutely unavoidable.

For example, the Dynamic Meditation – it is absolutely necessary for the modern man, although it may not have been at that time. If people are innocent, there is no need for Dynamic Meditation. But if people are repressed psychologically, are carrying a lot of burden, then they need catharsis. So Dynamic Meditation is just to help them clean the place. And then they can use any method, it will not be difficult. If they try directly right now, they will fail. I have seen many people trying directly and reaching nowhere, because they are so full of garbage that first it has to be emptied out.

Dynamic Meditation is of immense help. All the techniques that I have developed are for the contemporary man, and by doing these techniques he will be clean, unburdened, simple, innocent. So, the first thing is something cathartic, which is absolutely necessary for the contemporary man. And then those silent methods can be used.

Part One

No Commandments,
Just a Few Requests

My whole teaching is whole-oriented. I say 'be whole', I don't say 'be perfect'. And the difference is tremendous. When I say 'be whole', I allow you contradictions – then be wholly contradictory. When I say 'be whole', I don't give you a goal, a criterion, an ideal; I don't want to create any anxiety in you. I simply want you, in this moment, wherever, whatsoever you are doing, and whatsoever you are, to be total in it. If you are sad, be totally sad – you are whole. If you are angry, be totally angry. Go into it totally.

The idea of perfection is absolutely different, diametrically opposite – not even different, opposite. The perfectionist will say, 'Never be angry; always be compassionate. Never be sad; always be happy.' He chooses one polarity against the other.

In wholeness, we accept both the polarities: the lows and the highs, the ups and the downs.

Wholeness is totality.

The Invitation

I cannot give you any commandments. That would be insulting to you, it would be humiliating to you. That would be taking away your integrity, your freedom, your responsibility. No, I cannot commit such a criminal act. I can request you, I can invite you, to share with me my experience. I can become the host for you, and you can be the guest. It is an invitation, a welcome – but it is not a commandment.

What requests can I make of you?

It will look a little strange because Moses, Jesus, Mohammed, Krishna, Mahavira, Buddha – nobody requests you. They all have orders for you: 'Follow, or fall into hell.' They don't give you any chance even to think. They reduce your very existence, your very being, to an object. They don't respect your individuality. Hence I see something irreligious in all those people. They are special; somebody is special because he has seen God with his own eyes. Now, in what way can you be equal to him? By what right can you question him? He has seen God himself, talked to him. He has brought the message to you; he is the messenger. Somebody is the only begotten son of God – now, what can you do about it? You cannot be equal to Jesus. All that you can do is to follow, to imitate, to be a psychological slave, which is a far more dangerous slavery than any other.

Economic slavery is nothing compared to psychological slavery. And all these people who have been giving commandments, disciplines, showing you the way to live, what to eat, what to wear, what to do, what not to do – all these people are in some way trying to make you a psychological slave. I cannot call these people religious.

To me, religion begins with psychological freedom.

I cannot give you commandments, but I can give you a few requests. Nobody has done it before, so it may look a little outlandish, but what can I do? I can give you a few invitations.

DON'T LET YOUR DOUBT DIE

That is the most precious thing you have, because it is doubt that one day is going to help you discover the truth. All these people say, 'Believe!' Their first effort is to destroy your doubt. Start with faith, because if you don't start with faith, on each step you will raise questions. Hence I would like it to be my first request to you: doubt until you discover. Do not believe until you come to know yourself. Once you believe, you will never be able to know on your own. Belief is poison, the most dangerous poison there is, because it kills your doubt; it kills your inquiry; it takes away from you your most precious instrument.

Whatever science has achieved in 300 years is through doubt. And in 10,000 years, religion has achieved nothing because of its belief. You can see, anybody who has eyes can see, that in 300 years science has achieved so much, in spite of all the hindrances created by the religious people. What has been the basic power of science? It was doubt.

Doubt, and go on doubting until you come to a point that you cannot doubt anymore. And you cannot doubt anymore only when you come to know something on your own. Then there is no question of doubt, there is no way to doubt.

NEVER IMITATE

The mind is an imitator, because imitation is very easy. To *be* someone is very difficult. To *become* someone is very easy – all you need is to be a hypocrite, which is not much of a problem. Deep down you remain the same, but on the surface you go on painting yourself according to some image. The Christian is trying to become like Christ – that's what the word *Christian* means. You would love to be like Christ; you are on the way, maybe far away, but moving slowly. A Christian means a person trying slowly to become a Christ, a Mohammedan means a person trying to become Mohammed. But unfortunately, this is not possible; this is not in the very nature of the universe. It only creates unique beings. It has no idea at all of carbon copies, duplicates, photocopied material; existence has no idea – just the original. And each individual is so unique and original that if he tries to become Christ, he is committing suicide. If he tries to become a Buddha, he is committing suicide.

So the second request is: Don't imitate. If you want to know who you are, please avoid imitation, that's a way of avoiding knowing yourself.

You cannot change the universal laws. You can only be yourself, and nothing else. And it is beautiful to be yourself. Anything original has beauty, freshness, fragrance, aliveness. Anything that is imitated is dead, dull, phony, plastic. You can pretend, but whom are you deceiving? Except yourself, you are not deceiving anybody. And what is the point of deceiving? What are you going to gain?

Thousands of people are living, even today, along the guidelines of Buddha. Those guidelines may have been good for Gautam Buddha, he may have enjoyed it; I have no quarrel with him. But he was not imitating anybody! That you don't see at all. Is Christ trying to imitate anybody? If you have just a little intelligence, a very little intelligence, that will do; it is not that you need genius to understand the simple fact. Whom has Christ imitated?

Whom has Buddha imitated? Whom has Lao Tzu imitated? Nobody! That's why they have flowered. But you are imitating.

The first thing to learn is that non-imitation is one of the fundamentals of religious life. Don't be a Christian and don't be a Mohammedan and don't be a Hindu – so that you can discover who you are. But before discovering, instead you start covering yourself with all kinds of labels, and then you go on reading those labels, and thinking this is you – you are a Mohammedan, you are a Christian. And those are labels glued upon you, by yourself or by your parents, by your well-wishers. They are all your enemies. Whoever tries to distract you from your being is your enemy. This is my definition. Whoever helps you to remain yourself – determinedly, whatever the cost, whatever the consequence – is your friend.

BEWARE OF KNOWLEDGE

It is so cheap to become knowledgeable. Scriptures are there, libraries are there, universities are there; it is so easy to become knowledgeable. And once you become knowledgeable, you are in a very sensitive space, because the ego would like to believe that this is *your* knowledge – and not only knowledgeability, it is your wisdom. The ego would like to change knowledge into wisdom. You will start believing that you know.

You know nothing. You know only books and what is written in the books. Perhaps those books are written by people just like you. Ninety-nine percent of books are written by other bookish people. In fact, if you read ten books, your mind becomes so full of rubbish that you would like to pour it down into the eleventh book. What else are you going to do with it? You have to unburden yourself.

I have been a professor in two universities, and I have watched hundreds of professors. That is the most snobbish tribe in the whole world. The professor thinks himself to be a different species altogether, because he *knows*. And what does he know? Just words, and words are not experience. You can go on repeating the word love, love, love, millions of times; then too it won't give you the taste of love. But if you read books on love – and there are thousands of books on love, novels and poetries, stories, treatises, theses – you can come to know so much about love that you may forget completely that you have never loved, that you don't know what love is all about.

So the third thing is to beware of knowledge, to be so alert that whenever you want, you can put your knowledge aside and it will not block your vision. It will not come between you and reality. You have to go to reality utterly naked. But if there are so many books between you and reality, then what you see will not be the real. It will be distorted by your books in so many ways, so by the time it reaches you it may have no connection at all with the reality.

LOVE

I will not say 'pray' because there is no God to pray to. I cannot say, like all the religions, that prayer will make you religious; it will give you a bogus religiousness. So the word *prayer* has to be completely dropped. God is not there, hence talking to the empty sky is utterly foolish. The danger is, you may start hearing voices from the sky; then you have gone beyond the limit of normality. Then you will need psychiatric treatment! So before that happens – before God answers you – please don't ask.

My word for prayer is *love*. Forget the word *prayer*, replace it with *love*. Love is not for some invisible God. Love is for the visible – human beings, animals, trees, oceans, mountains. Spread your wings of love as far and wide as you can.

And remember, love needs no belief system. Even the atheist loves, even the communist loves, even the material-ist loves. So love is something intrinsic to you – nothing imposed from outside, such that only a Christian can love, or only a Hindu can love – it is your human potential. And I would like you to depend on your human potential rather than these bogus conditionings of Christian, Jewish, Hindu. You don't bring them with you, but love you bring with you; it is part and parcel of your being. Love without any inhibition, without any taboos.

LIVE MOMENT TO MOMENT

Go on dying every moment to the past. It is finished. There is no need even to label it good or bad. The only thing to know is: it is finished, it is no more. It is going to be no more... gone and gone forever; now why waste time about it?

Never think of the past, because you are wasting the present, which is the only real thing in your hands. And never think of the future, because nobody knows how tomorrow is going to be, what tomorrow is going to be, how it is going to turn out, where you are going to land – you cannot imagine.

But this goes on happening every day – you don't take note of the fact that yesterday you wasted so much time planning for today, and it has not turned out to be according to your ideas and your plans, and this and that.

Now you are worried about why you wasted that time – and again you are wasting it!

Remain in the moment, true to the moment, utterly here now, as if there has been no yesterday and there is going to be no tomorrow – only then can you be here now totally. And that totality of being in the present joins you with existence, because existence knows no past, no future. It is always here now.

Existence knows only one tense, and that is the present tense. It is language that creates three tenses, and creates 3,000 tensions in your mind. Existence knows only one tense, and that is present: and it is not a tension at all, it is utterly relaxing. When you are totally here, no yesterdays pulling you back and no tomorrows pulling you somewhere else, you are relaxed.

To me, to be in the moment is meditation, to be utterly in the moment. And then it is so beautiful, so fragrant, so fresh. It never gets old. It never goes anywhere.

It is we who come and pass; existence remains as it is. It is not time that passes, it is we who come and pass. But it is a fallacy: rather than seeing that we are passing, we have created a great invention, the clock – 'time passes'.

Just think, if there is no human being on the earth will there be any time passing? The ocean will still be coming to the beach, crashing its waves on the rocks.

The sun will rise, the sun will set, but there will be no morning, there will be no evening. There will be no time as such. Time is a mind invention, and basically time can exist only with yesterdays and tomorrows; the present moment is not part of time.

When you are simply here, just now, there is no time. You are breathing, you are alive, you are feeling, you are open to everything that is happening all around.

BE JUST AN AUTHENTIC HUMAN BEING

In existence there is no hierarchy: nobody is lower, nobody is higher. Everybody is just himself. Some tree is tall, some tree is not tall. That does not mean that the tall tree is greater, superior, and the small tree is not greater, not superior. No, in nature there is no hierarchy. The small tree has the potential of being a small tree. It has brought its potential to its completion; it is happy, blissful. It is not comparing itself with the tall tree. And the tall tree is not looking downwards with the eyes of a president looking at the ordinary people, or a prime minister looking at the ordinary people. The tall tree is just a tall tree. It has fulfilled its potential. Both have done exactly the same; whatsoever was their potential, they have brought it to fulfillment... and fulfillment is bliss. What you fulfill does not matter.

Fulfillment of your potential is bliss.

So remember: Accept your humanity with joy, as a gift of existence – not that you are expelled from the Garden of Eden, not that it is a punishment, not that you have to repent.

Jesus goes on saying, 'Repent! Repent!' For what? Because Adam and Eve ate an apple? And we have to repent for it? Now my doctor does not allow me, but for my whole life I have been eating apples, at least six per day. That was my main diet. If anybody has committed the original sin, I am here! That poor Adam and Eve... just one apple. And they must have each eaten only half; or perhaps the serpent also had some share in it. I don't know, because the people who create these stories don't give any clue. Just a small fragment and they think it is enough.

We are still in the Garden of Eden. That's what I want you to understand. This existence is the Garden of Eden, there is no other Garden of Eden. We are already in it. And how can one be expelled from existence? Just look at the absurdity of the idea. Even if God wants to, he cannot expel anybody from existence. Where will he expel him to? Wherever he expels him to, it will be existence still – and his creation still. And whatever God creates must be holy – or does he also create unholy things? So even if he expels you, you will still be walking on the holy earth, the holy planet.

There is no point in the story. It is just to keep you tethered to the idea that unless you undo what Adam has done, you will never rise above your humanity. And what has Adam done? He has disobeyed. Rather than listening to God, he listened to the devil. Of course, the devil was more logical, more appealing, more convincing.

This God, the God of this story, seems to have no guts. If the devil had convinced Adam and Eve, the God could have argued with them. That would have been far more gentlemanly than driving them out of the Garden of Eden. Why was he so angry? And if he was angry, he should have been angry at the serpent, at the devil – not at these innocent people. But in the story, it seems the serpent still lives in the Garden of Eden. The story says nothing more about the serpent, so what happened? He still lives there!

To implant the idea that you are born in original sin, different methods have been used by different religions, but they have to make it certain that you are born in sin. That's why Jesus is born out of a virgin, because to be born out of sex is to be born out of sin. Sex is sin. Now, I again go on wondering how the Holy Ghost made the virgin Mary pregnant. I don't think he used artificial insemination. In what way did the poor woman become pregnant? But the

Christians have to make poor Jesus a bastard, just to keep him away from the sin of sex. Everybody else is born out of sex, is born out of sin – only Jesus is not born that way. Jesus is special.

Why these foolish stories? Just to make the person special, different from you. It is just to humiliate you. It is disgusting! How humanity has been insulted by all the religions! It is time that people say, 'Stop all this nonsense. There is no superman, and there has never been one – we are all human beings. And these stories are all imaginary, hocus pocus.'

DON'T FIGHT WITH YOUR BODY

All the religions have been teaching you to fight against nature. Whatsoever is natural is condemned. The religions say that you have to manage to do something unnatural, only then can you get out of the imprisonment of biology, physiology, psychology, all the walls that surround you. But if you go on in harmony with your body, with your mind, with your heart, then the religions say you will never be able to go beyond you. That's where I oppose all the religions. They have put a poisonous seed in your being, so you live in the body, but you don't love your body.

The body serves you for 70, 80, 90, even 100 years, and

there is no other mechanism that science has been able to invent that can be compared to the body. Its complexities, its miracles that it goes on doing for you... and you don't even say thank you. You treat your body as your enemy, and your body is your friend.

It takes care of you in every possible way, while you are awake, while you are asleep. Even in sleep it goes on taking care of you.

You go on eating all kinds of things without bothering what happens when you swallow them. You don't ask the body whether its mechanism, its chemistry, will be able to digest what you are eating. But somehow your inner chemistry goes on working for almost a century. It has an automatic system for replacing parts that have gone wrong. It goes on throwing them out, creating new parts; and you have to do nothing about it, it goes on happening on its own. The body has a certain wisdom of its own.

It is not your foe, it is your friend. It is a gift of nature to you. It is part of nature. It is joined with nature in every possible way. You are bridged not only with breathing; with sunrays you are bridged, with the fragrance of flowers you are bridged, with the moonlight you are bridged. You are bridged from everywhere; you are not a separate island. Drop that idea. You are part of this whole continent, and yet... it has given you an individuality. This is what I call a miracle.

You are part and parcel of existence, yet you have an individuality. Existence has done a miracle, has made possible something impossible. So, being in harmony with your body, you will be in harmony with nature, with existence. Instead of going against the current, go with the current. Be in a let-go. Allow life to happen. Don't force anything, in any good name. For the sake of some holy book, for the sake of some holy ideal, don't disturb your harmony.

Nothing is more valuable than to be harmonious, in accord with the whole.

LIVE, AND TRY TO KNOW WHAT LIFE IS

All the religions are agreed upon one point – that real life begins after death. This life is only a rehearsal, not the real drama. The real drama will happen after death. Here, you are only preparing for the drama. So sacrifice everything to get ready for the drama that is going to happen after death. They teach sacrifice. Sacrifice love, sacrifice life, sacrifice joy, sacrifice everything. The more you sacrifice, the more you will be capable of participating in the drama, the great drama, after death. They have tried to focus your mind on life after death.

One man was asking me – he was one of the richest

men of India, Sahu Shanti Prasad; we were walking in his big garden, and he asked me, 'I always wanted to ask you what happens after death.'

I said, 'Are you alive or not?'

He said, 'What kind of question is this? I am alive.'

I said, 'You are alive. Do you know what life is?'

He said, 'That I cannot answer. Honestly, I don't know.'

I said, 'You are alive, and you don't even know what life is? How can you know death when you are not dead yet? So wait. While you are alive, try to know life; and soon you will be dead, then in your grave you can contemplate about death. Nobody will be bothering you. But why are you concerned what happens after death? Why are you not concerned what happens before death? That should be the real concern. When death comes, we will face it, we will see it, we will see what it is. I am not dead, so how can I say? You will have to ask somebody who is dead what happens. I am alive. I can tell you what life is, and I can tell you how to know what life is.'

'But,' he said, 'all the religious teachers I go to listen to talk about death; nobody talks about life.'

They are not interested in life, in fact; they want you all not to be interested in life. Their business depends on your interest in death. And about death, the most beautiful thing is that you can create any kind of fiction and nobody can argue against it. Neither you can prove it, nor can anybody disprove it. And if you are a believer, then of course all your scriptures are in support of the priest, the monk, the rabbi, and he can quote those scriptures.

Don't be bothered about death, heaven and hell, and this goddamned God. You simply remain with the life that is dancing in you, breathing in you, alive in you. You have to come closer to yourself to know it. Perhaps you are standing too far away from yourself. Your concerns have taken you far away. You have to come back home.

So remember that while you are alive it is so precious – don't miss a single moment. Squeeze the whole juice of it, and that juice will give you the taste of the existential, and that will be a revelation of all that is hidden from you and will remain hidden from you.

RESPECT LIFE, REVERE LIFE

There is nothing more holy than life, nothing more divine than life. And life does not consist of big things. Those religious fools have been telling you, 'Do big things,' and life consists of small things. The strategy is clear. They tell you, 'Do big things, something great, something that your name will be remembered for afterwards. Do something great.' And of course it appeals to the ego. The ego is the agent of the priest. All the churches and all the synagogues and all the temples have only one agent, and that is the ego – do something great, something big.

I want to tell you, there is nothing big, nothing great. Life consists of very small things. So if you become interested in so-called big things, you will be missing life.

Life consists of sipping a cup of tea, of gossiping with a friend; going for a morning walk, not going anywhere in particular, just for a walk, no goal, no end, from any point you can turn back; cooking food for someone you love; cooking food for yourself, because you love your body, too; washing your clothes, cleaning the floor, watering the garden... these small things, very small things... saying hello to a stranger, which was not needed at all because there was no question of any business with the stranger.

The man who can say hello to a stranger can also say hello to a flower, can also say hello to the tree, can sing a song to the birds. They sing every day and you have not bothered at all that some day you should return the call. Just small things, very small things....

And I am not talking about going to the synagogue – that is a big thing. Going to the church – that is a big thing; leave all that to fools. There are many, and they also need some kind of engagement, occupation; those synagogues and churches and temples provide it. But to you, existence, nothing but existence, is the only temple.

Nothing but life is the only God I teach you. Respect your life. Out of that respect you will start respecting life in others.

BE CREATIVE

Only a creative person can know what bliss is. Paint, play music, compose poetry, do anything, not for any other purpose, just for your joy, for no other reason. If you can compose poetry just for your own joy, or a few friends may share it; if you can make a beautiful garden, just for the sheer joy of making it, and anybody who passes by may stand for a while and have a look – that's enough reward.

But this is my experience, that only creative people know what bliss is. Those who are not creative cannot know bliss.

They can know happiness, and I will have to make the difference clear to you. Happiness is always caused by something: you get a Nobel prize, you are happy; you are rewarded, you are happy; you become the champion of something and you are happy. Something causes it, but it depends on others. The Nobel prize will be decided by the Nobel committee. The gold medal will be decided by the gold medal committee, the university. It depends on others. And if you have been working for this motive – that you want to attain the Nobel prize and you are writing poetry, novels, just in order to get the Nobel prize – while you are working, it will be just a drag. There will be no bliss, because your happiness is there, far away, in the hands of the Nobel prize committee. And even if you get the Nobel prize, it is going to be just a momentary thing. How long can you go on bragging about it?

Bliss is something totally different. It is not dependent on anybody. It is the joy of creating something; whether anybody appreciates it or not is irrelevant. You enjoyed it while you were making it – that's enough, more than enough.

BE ORDINARY

Everybody wants to be extraordinary, that is very ordinary. But to be ordinary and just relax in being ordinary, that is superbly extraordinary. One who can accept his ordinariness without any grudge, any grumbling – with joy, because this is how the whole existence is – then nobody can destroy his bliss. Nobody can steal it, nobody can take it away. Then wherever you are you will be in bliss.

I was in New Delhi, and after I had spoken a man stood up and asked me, 'What do you think about yourself? Will you be going to heaven or hell?'

I said, 'As far as I know, there are no such things. But if by chance they are there, I can only hope for hell.'

He said, 'What!'

I said, 'In hell you will find all the colorful people – ordinary people, but all colorful. In heaven you will find great scholars, theologians, saints, philosophers – but all serious, all quarreling, all against each other, disputing continuously. It must be a quarrelsome place, where you cannot find a moment of silence. As far as I understand, if God has any intelligence, he must have escaped to hell, because that is the only place where nobody is going to argue about stupid, silly things, where people will be simply enjoying, dancing, singing, eating, sleeping, working.'

I said to him, 'To me, the ordinary is the most extraordinary phenomenon in existence.'

THE GOLDEN RULE FOR LIFE IS THAT THERE ARE NO GOLDEN RULES

There cannot be. Life is so vast, so immense, so strange, mysterious, it cannot be reduced into a rule or a maxim. All maxims fall short, are too small; they cannot contain life and its living energies. Hence the golden rule is significant, that there are no golden rules.

An authentic human being does not live by rules, maxims, commandments. That's the way of the pseudo. The authentic human being simply lives. Yes, if you ask an authentic man, he may tell you about certain rules, but they are not the rules that he has followed himself. He has just found them on the way of living, just like collecting seashells on the beach. He had not gone to collect the seashells, he had gone to enjoy the early morning, the fresh air, the sun, the sea, the sand. Just by the way, he found those seashells.

Anybody living according to a rule is destroying himself, poisoning himself, because the rule was found by somebody who was not you, somewhere where you will never be, in some time, in some space that is not your time and not your space. It is very dangerous to follow that rule. You will be distracting your life from its center, its grounding – you will misshape yourself. Trying to shape yourself you will only misshape yourself, disfigure yourself.

So all the rules I have talked about – you have to remember that before all of them comes the golden rule.

LIVE DANGEROUSLY

What does it mean exactly? It simply means that in life there are always alternatives. You are always at a crossroads, always and always. Each moment is a crossroads, and you have to choose where you are going, what is going to be your path; each moment you have to choose. Each moment is decisive because you are discarding many ways and choosing one.

Now, if you choose the comfortable, the convenient, then you will never be able to live intensely. The comfortable, the convenient, the conventional, which the society approves, means that you are ready to become a psychological slave. That's why all this convenience.... The society will give you everything, if you give your freedom to it. It will give you respectability, it will give you great posts in the hierarchy, in the bureaucracy – but you have to drop one thing: your freedom, your individuality. You have to become a number in the crowd. The crowd hates the person who is not part of it. The crowd becomes very tense seeing a stranger amongst it, because the stranger becomes a question mark.

You have been living a certain life, a certain style, a certain religion, a certain politics. You have been following the way of the mob, and you were very comfortable, cozy, because those surrounding you were all people just like you. What you were doing, they were doing. Everybody else was doing the same; that gave the feeling that you were doing the right thing. So many people could not be wrong. And in gratitude that you are following them, they give you respectability, honor. Your ego is fulfilled. Life is convenient, but it is flat. You live horizontally – a very thin slice of life, just like a slice of bread cut very thin. In a linear way you live.

To live dangerously means to live vertically.

Each moment then has a depth and a height. It touches the highest star and the deepest bottom. It knows nothing of the horizontal line. But then you are a stranger in the crowd, then you are behaving differently from everybody else. And this creates an unease in people, for the simple reason that they are not enjoying their life, they have not lived their life, they have not taken the responsibility to live it, they have not risked anything to have it – but because everybody else was also like them, the question was not arising.

But this stranger comes who lives in a different way, behaves in a different way, and suddenly something is stirred in them. Their repressed life, which is like a spring, forcibly repressed, suddenly starts stirring, starts creating questions that this way too is possible. And this man seems to be having a different shine to his eyes, a different joy around him. He walks, sits, stands, not like everybody else. Something is unique about him. But the most impressive thing about him is he seems to be utterly contented, blissful – as if he has arrived. You are all wandering and he has arrived. Now, this man is a danger to the crowd. The crowd will kill him.

It is not a coincidence that people like Socrates are poisoned. What was the trouble with the man? He was such a unique genius, that if Greece had produced only Socrates, that would have been enough to make history, enough to be remembered forever. But the crowd could not tolerate this man. He was a very simple man, absolutely harmless. They poisoned and killed him. What was his crime? His crime was, he was an individual. He walked on his own path, not on the superhighway where everybody is moving. He was going through a labyrinth of his own. And the society soon became afraid because a few people started moving away from the highway to find their own ways.

Socrates was saying that you cannot walk on a way made by others for you. You have to walk, and make your road by walking. It is not that roads are made available to you readymade, you have simply to walk – no. You have to create the road by walking; just as you walk, you create the road. And remember, it is only for you, not for anybody else. It is just like the birds flying in the sky leave no trace for any other bird to follow. The sky remains empty again. Any bird can fly, but he will have to make his own way.

Socrates is not asking to be accepted. Socrates is saying, 'Please leave me alone – just as I leave you alone. Please allow my freedom. I don't trespass on your life, you should not trespass on my life.' It seems to be absolutely honest. He is not asking to be accepted. He is not saying, 'Whatever I am saying is true, and you have to accept it.' No, he is saying, 'Whatsoever I am saying, it is my right to say. You have your right to say.'

The judges were a little guilty when they decided this man should be killed. He was the best flowering of Greek genius. So they offered him a few alternatives; they said, 'One thing is, you can leave Athens....' In those days Greece was composed of city democracies, and that is really a far more democratic way. The smaller the unit, the more democracy is possible, because it is direct democracy.

The people of Athens used to gather, raise their hands for or against, and decide things. Now, in a country like America the democracy becomes so indirect, and the person you choose... once you have chosen him for a few years then you don't know what he is going to do. During those few years you cannot control him. He may have promised you something and he may do just the opposite. Exactly that is what goes on happening. But in Athens it was a direct democracy. Any important issue, and the people of Athens would be together there and they would vote for it or against it. So the power was not delegated for five years, it was always in the hands of the people.

So the judges said, 'It is very simple: leave Athens. You can make your home in any other city, and wherever you are you will find disciples, friends – about that there is no question.'

Socrates said, 'It is not a question of surviving. What you are saying is certainly convenient, and any business-man would have chosen that. It is simple. Why unnecessarily get killed? Move to another town.' Socrates said, 'I'm not going out of Athens because it is a question of choosing between convenience or life, and I choose life – even if it brings death. But I will not choose convenience; that is cowardly.'

They offered him another alternative. They said, 'Then do one thing: remain in Athens, but stop teaching.'

He said, 'That is even more difficult. You are asking birds not to sing in the morning, trees not to blossom when it is time to blossom? You are asking me not to speak the truth? And that is my only joy: to share my truth with those who are groping in the dark. I am going to be here and I am going to continue teaching the truth.'

The judges said, 'Then we are helpless, because the mob, with a majority, wants you to be poisoned and killed.'

He said, 'That's perfectly okay. You can kill me, but you

cannot kill my spirit....' But remember, by spirit he does not mean soul. By spirit he means his courage, his devotion to truth, his way of life. You cannot change that. He said, 'You can kill me. And about death I am not worried at all, because there are only two alternatives. Either I will simply die, so there is no problem then. When I am not, what problem can there be? So either I simply die, then there is no problem, or I don't die and my soul goes on living. Then at least I will have the satisfaction that I was not a coward, that I stuck to my truth, that you could kill me, but you could not bend me.'

He died joyously. The death scene of Socrates is something beautiful in the whole history of man. In Greece it was not a cross; it was poison that had to be given. So outside the man was preparing the poison, the official poisoner who gives the poison to people who are sentenced to death. Six in the evening was the time. The sun was setting and Socrates asked again and again, 'What is the matter? Ask that man; it is getting late.'

And the poisoner was really trying to make it as late as possible. He had loved this man and he wanted him to live a little longer. That much he could make possible... he could go on preparing the poison, slowly. But disciples came again and again and they said, 'The master is asking why you are late.'

With tears in his eyes, he said, 'He is really a dangerous man. I am trying to give him a little longer to live, but he is in a hurry.'

The poisoner asked Socrates, 'Why are you in a hurry?'

He said, 'I am in a hurry because life I have lived tremendously, totally; I know it. Death is unknown; it is a great adventure. I would like to taste death.'

Now, you cannot kill such a man. There is no way to kill such a man, who wants to taste death, who wants to know death, who wants to jump into the challenge and the adventure of the unknown.

Living dangerously means whenever there are alternatives, beware: don't choose the convenient, the comfortable, the respectable, the socially acceptable, the honorable. Choose something that rings a bell in your heart. Choose something that you would like to do in spite of any consequences.

The coward thinks of consequences: 'If I do this, what will happen? What will be the result?' He is more concerned about the result.

The real man never thinks of the consequences. He thinks only of the act, in this moment. He feels, 'This is what is appealing to me, and I am going to do it.' Then whatever happens is welcome. He will never regret. A real man never regrets, never repents, because he has never done anything against himself. The coward dies thousands of times before death, and continuously regrets, repents: it would have been better if he had done that, married that man, that woman, chosen that profession, gone to that college.... Thousands of alternatives are always there, and you cannot do them all.

The society teaches you, 'Choose the convenient, the comfortable; choose the well-trodden path where your fore-fathers and their forefathers and their forefathers, since Adam and Eve, have been walking. Choose the well-trodden path. That is a proof: so many millions of people have passed on it, you cannot go wrong.' But remember one thing, the crowd has never had the experience of truth.

Truth has only happened to individuals.

The well-trodden path is not trodden by Socrates and people like Socrates. It is trodden by the mass, the mediocre, the people who have no courage to go into the unknown. They never get off the highway. They keep clinging to each other because that gives them a certain satisfaction, consolation: 'So many people are with us....'

That's why all the religions continuously go on trying to make more and more converts. The reason is not that they are interested in people and their life and their transforma-tion – no, they themselves are not transformed – but if you have more Christians than Hindus, naturally it seems you have better chances of having truth with you than the Hindus. If the Buddhists are more than the Christians, then of course they can go on believing that they have the truth, that's why so many people are with them.

But I want you to remember, truth has always happened to individuals. It is not a collective phenomenon, it does not happen to a crowd. It always happens to the individual. It is just like love. Have you seen a crowd in love? That is impossible... that a crowd falls in love with another crowd. At least up to now it has not happened. It is an individual phenomenon. One person falls in love with another person. But in love at least there are two persons. In truth, even two are not there. You alone, in your absolute aloneness, experience it.

Truth comes only to the rebellious, and to be a rebel is certainly to live dangerously.

Living dangerously means: don't put stupid conditions between you and life – comfort, convenience, respectability. Drop all these things, and allow life to happen to you, and go with it without bothering whether you are on the highway or not, without bothering where you are going to end. Only very few people live. Ninety-nine point nine percent of people only slowly commit suicide.

And the last thing to remember – because that is so absolutely essential I should not be forgiven for forgetting it:

LIVE WATCHFULLY

Whatsoever you are doing – walking, sitting, eating, or if you are not doing anything, just breathing, resting, relaxing in the grass, never forget that you are a watcher.

You will forget it again and again. You will get involved in some thought, some feeling, some emotion, some sentiment – anything will distract you from the watcher. Remember, and run back to your center of watching. Make it an inner process continuously.... You will be surprised at how life changes its whole quality. I can move my hand without any watchfulness, and I can also move my hand absolutely watching from inside the whole movement. The movements are totally different. The first movement is a robot movement, mechanical. The second movement is a conscious movement. And when you are conscious you feel that hand from within; when you are not conscious you only know the hand from without.

You have known your face only in the mirror, from the without, because you are not a watcher. If you start watching, you will feel your face from within – and that is such an experience, to watch yourself from within. Then, slowly, strange things start happening. Thoughts disappear, feelings disappear, emotions disappear, and there is a silence surrounding you. You are just like an island in the middle of the ocean of silence... just a watcher, as if a flame of light at the center of your being, radiating the whole of your being.

In the beginning it will only be an inner experience. Slowly you will see that radiation spreading out of your body, those rays reaching other people. You will be surprised and shocked that other people, if they are a little bit sensitive, will immediately become aware that something has touched them that was not visible.

For example, if you are watching yourself.... Just walk behind somebody, watching yourself, and it is almost certain the person will turn and look back suddenly, for no reason. When you are watching yourself, your watchfulness starts radiating, and it is bound to touch the person who is ahead of you. And if he is touched by something that is invisible, he is going to look back: 'What is the matter?' And you are that far away, you cannot even touch him with your hand.

You can try that experiment: somebody is sleeping and you can sit by their side, just watching yourself, and the person will suddenly wake up, open his eyes and look all around as if somebody has touched him.

Slowly you will also become able to feel the touch through the rays. That is what is called the 'vibe.' It is not a nonexistential thing. The other person feels it; you will also feel that you have touched the other person.

The English phrase, being 'touched,' is used very significantly. You may use it without understanding what it means when you say 'I was touched' by the person. He may not have said a single word to you. He may have just passed by. He may have just looked once at your eyes, and you feel 'touched' by the person. It is not just a word – it actually happens. And then those rays go on spreading to people, to animals, to trees, to rocks... and one day you will see, you are touching the whole universe from within.

This is the experience I call the experience of godliness.

Part Two

Ordinary Enlightenment for Extraordinary Times

Man could have grown to immense heights, to the Himalayan peaks of consciousness, but because of the unconscious, stupid majority of people, evolution is delayed continually.

You kill one Socrates, you have delayed evolution perhaps for 1,000 years. You kill a Buddha by poisoning, you have again delayed evolution for another 1,000 years. You kill al-Hillaj Mansoor and you have delayed evolution. Evolution is being delayed continually, because the majority cannot tolerate anybody rising like an Everest – the highest peak of the Himalayas – in consciousness, in love, in compassion.

We have to create a great force of thousands of Buddhas. Only then there is a possibility of a quantum leap in evolution.

Belief is Borrowed,
Trust is Yours

Trust is possible only if first you trust in yourself. The most fundamental thing has to happen within you first. If you trust in yourself you can trust in existence. But if you don't trust in yourself then no other trust is ever possible.

And the society destroys trust at the very roots. It does not allow you to trust yourself. It teaches all other kinds of trust – trust in the parents, trust in the church, trust in the state, trust in God, *ad infinitum*. But the basic trust is completely destroyed. And then all other trusts are phony, are bound to be phony. Then all other trusts are just plastic flowers. You don't have real roots for real flowers to grow.

The society does it deliberately, on purpose, because a man who trusts in himself is dangerous for the society – a society that depends on slavery, a society that has invested too much in slavery.

A man trusting himself is an independent man. You cannot make predictions about him, he will move in his own way. Freedom will be his life. He will trust when he feels, when he loves, and then his trust will have a tremendous intensity and truth in it. Then his trust will be alive and authentic. And he will be ready to risk all for his trust – but only when he feels it, only when it is true, only when it stirs his heart, only when it stirs his intelligence and his love, otherwise not. You cannot force him into any kind of believing.

— ❀ —

Belief is theoretical.

Trust is existential.

You can change your belief without any trouble; it is just like changing your clothes. From a Hindu, you can become a Christian; from a Christian, you can become a Mohammedan; from a Mohammedan, you can become a communist. There is no problem, because belief is only of the mind. If anything is more convincing, more logical, you can change it. It has no roots in your heart.

Belief is like plastic flowers, which look like flowers from far away. They don't have any roots, they don't need any care – no manure, no chemicals, no watering, no gardening, nothing is needed. And they are permanent people, they can remain with you your whole life long – because they were never born, so they will never die. They are manufactured. Unless you destroy them, they will remain.

Trust is a real rose. It has roots, and roots go deep into your heart and into your being.

Belief is just in the head.

Trust is in the heart, in your deeper world of being. To change trust is almost impossible – it has never happened, it is not known to have happened in the whole of history. If you trust, you trust; there is no possibility of its changing.

And it goes on growing because it has roots. It never remains static; it is dynamic, it is a living force, it goes on growing new foliage, new flowers, new branches.

The most difficult thing in life is to drop the past – because to drop the past means to drop the whole identity, to drop the whole personality. It is to drop yourself. You are nothing but your past, you are nothing but your conditionings.

It is not like dropping clothes – it is as if one's skin is being peeled off. Your past is all that you know you are. Dropping is difficult, arduous – the most difficult thing in life. But those who can dare to drop it, only they live. Others simply pretend to live, others simply go on dragging themselves somehow. They don't have any vitality – they can't have. They live at the minimum, and to live at the minimum is to miss the whole thing.

It is only when you live at the optimum of your potential that blossoming happens. It is only at the optimum expression of your being, of your truth, that God arrives – that you start feeling the presence of the divine.

The more you disappear, the more you feel the presence of the divine. But the presence will be felt only later on. The first condition to be fulfilled is disappearing. It is a kind of death.

Hence it is difficult. And conditioning has gone very deep – because you have been conditioned from the very beginning; from the first moment you were born, conditioning started. By the time you became alert, a little aware, it had already reached to the deepest core of your being. Unless you penetrate yourself to this deepest core that was not conditioned at all, that was before conditioning started, unless you become that silent and that innocent, you will never know who you are.

You will know you are a Hindu, a Christian, a communist. You will know you are an Indian, a Chinese, a Japanese, and you will know many things – but those things are just conditionings imposed upon you. You had come into the world utterly silent, pure, innocent. Your innocence was absolute.

Meditation means to penetrate to that core, to that innermost core. Zen people call it knowing the 'original face.'

Everybody is born as one single individual, but by the time he is mature enough to participate in life he has become a crowd. If you just sit silently and listen to your mind, you will find so many voices. You will be surprised, you can recognize those voices very well. Some voice is from your grandfather, some voice is from your grandmother, some voice is from your father, some voice is from your mother, some voice is from the priest, from the teacher, from the neighbors, from your friends, from your enemies. All these voices are jumbled up in a crowd within you, and if you want to find your own voice, it is almost impossible; the crowd is too thick.

In fact, you have forgotten your own voice long before. You were never given freedom enough to voice your opinions. You were always taught obedience. You were taught to say yes to everything that your elders were saying to you. You were taught that you have to follow whatever your teachers or your priests are doing. Nobody ever told you to search for your own voice – 'Have you got any voice of your own or not?'

So your voice has remained very subdued and other voices are very loud, very commanding, because they were orders and you had followed them – in spite of yourself. You had no intention to follow, you could see that this is not right. But one has to be obedient to be respected, to be acceptable, to be loved.

Naturally only one voice is missing in you, only one person is missing in you, and that is you; otherwise there is a whole crowd. And that crowd is constantly driving you mad, because one voice says, 'Do this,' another voice says,

'Never do that! Don't listen to that voice!' And you are torn apart.

This whole crowd has to be withdrawn. This whole crowd has to be told, 'Now please leave me alone!' The people who have gone to the mountains or to the secluded forests were really not going away from the society; they were trying to find a place where they can disperse their crowd inside. And those people who have made a place within you are obviously reluctant to leave.

But if you want to become an individual in your own right, if you want to get rid of this continuous conflict and this mess within you, then you have to say goodbye to them – even when they belong to your respected father, your mother, your grandfather. It does not matter to whom they belong. One thing is certain: they are not your voices. They are the voices of people who have lived in their time, and they had no idea what the future was going to be. They have loaded their children with their own experience; their experience is not going to match with the unknown future.

They are thinking they are helping their children to be knowledgeable, to be wise, so their life can be easier and more comfortable, but they are doing just the wrong thing. With all the good intentions in the world, they are destroying the child's spontaneity, his own consciousness, his own ability to stand on his feet, and to respond to the new future which their old ancestors had no idea of.

He is going to face new storms, he is going to face new situations, and he needs a totally new consciousness to respond. Only then is his response going to be fruitful; only then can he have a victorious life, a life that is not just a long, long drawn-out despair, but a dance from moment to moment, which goes on becoming more and more deep to the last breath. He enters into death dancing, and joyously.

Be silent, and find your own self. Unless you find your own self, it is very difficult to disperse the crowd, because all those in the crowd are pretending, 'I am your self.' And you have no way to agree, or disagree.

So don't create any fight with the crowd. Let them fight amongst themselves – they are quite efficient in fighting amongst themselves. You, meanwhile, try to find yourself. And once you know who you are, you can just order them to get out of the house – it is actually that simple! But first you have to find yourself.

Once you are there, the master is there, the owner of the house is there. And all these people, who have been pretending to be masters themselves, start dispersing. The man who is himself, unburdened of the past, discontinuous with the past, original, strong as a lion and innocent as a child... he can reach to the stars, or even beyond the stars; his future is golden.

The Responsibility
of Being Free

Freedom is possible only when you are so integrated that you can take the responsibility of being free. The world is not free because people are not mature. Revolutionaries have been doing many things down through the centuries, but everything fails. Utopians have been continuously thinking of how to make man free, but nobody bothers – because man cannot be free unless he is integrated. Only a Buddha can be free, a Mahavira can be free, a Christ, a Mohammed can be free, a Zarathustra can be free, because freedom means the man now is aware. If you are not aware then the state is needed, the government is needed, the police is needed, the court is needed. Then freedom has to be cut from everywhere. Then freedom exists only in name; in fact it doesn't exist. How can freedom exist when governments exist? – it is impossible. But what to do?

If governments disappear, there will simply be anarchy. Freedom will not come in if governments disappear, there will simply be anarchy. It will be a worse state than it is now. It will be sheer madness. The police are needed because you are not alert. Otherwise, what is the point of having a policeman standing on the crossroad? If people are alert, the policeman can be removed, will have to be removed, because it is unnecessary. But people are not conscious.

So when I talk about freedom, I mean be responsible. The more responsible you become, the more free you become; or, the more free you become, the more responsibility comes on you. Then you have to be very alert to what you are doing, what you are saying. Even about your small unconscious gestures you have to be very alert – because there is nobody else to control you, it is only you. When I say to you that you are free, I mean that you are a God. It is not license, it is tremendous discipline.

Just to be free of society is not enough. To be free and responsible, to be free and responsibly free – only then are you free, otherwise you will be caught in another pattern. The drop-out is reacting, the people of Zen are rebelling. In reaction you just go to the opposite: if the society says no drugs, you say drugs are the only panacea. If the society says do this, you immediately do just the opposite. But remember, in doing the opposite, you are still in the trap of society because society has decided what you should do. Even the opposite is decided by society. The society said no drugs so you say, 'I am going to take drugs.' By saying no, the society has decided your direction.

So the one who is conventional is within the society,

and the one who has reacted against it again gets caught in the society. One says yes to the society, another says no to the society, but both react to the society. One who really wants to be free says neither yes nor no.

There are three kinds of freedom. One is 'freedom from'; that is a negative freedom: freedom from the father, freedom from the mother, freedom from the church, freedom from the society. That is a negative kind of freedom – freedom from – good in the beginning, but that can't be the goal. Once you are free from your parents, what are you going to do? Once you are free from your society then you will be at a loss. You will lose all meaning and significance because your whole life had meaning in saying 'no.' Now whom to say no to?

A young man came to me; he wanted to marry a girl. He was a *brahmin*, a very high-caste *brahmin*, very respected in the city, and he wanted to marry a Parsi girl. The parents were absolutely against it. They had told him that if he married that girl they would disown him – and he was the only son. The more stubborn the parents became, the more the young man became determined to marry the girl. He had come to ask my advice.

I said, 'Just meditate for three days on one thing: are you really interested in the girl or are you simply interested in saying no to your parents?'

He said, 'Why do you say this to me? I love the girl, I am absolutely in love!'

I said, 'If you say so, then get married. But I don't see any love in your eyes, I don't see any love in your heart. I don't see any fragrance of love. I only see some negative aura around you, a black aura around your face. It says you are determined to go against your parents – the girl is only an excuse.'

But he wouldn't listen. If he was not going to listen to his parents, how was he going to listen to me? He got married. After six months he came to see me, crying and weeping. He fell at my feet and said, 'You were right – I don't love that woman, that love was false. You were right, your diagnosis was right. Now that I have got married to her and I have denied my parents' order, all love has disappeared.'

This is 'freedom from.' This is not much of a freedom, but better than nothing.

The second kind of freedom is 'freedom for' – that is positive freedom. Your interest is not in denying something, rather you want to create something. For example, you want to be a poet, and just because you want to be a poet you have to say no to your parents. But your basic orientation is that you want to be a poet and your parents would like you to be a plumber. 'Better be a plumber! That is far more paying, far more economical, far more respectable, too. Poet?! People will think you are crazy! And how are you going to live? And how are you going to support your wife and your children? Poetry doesn't pay!'

But if you are for poetry, ready to risk all, this is a higher freedom, better than the first. It is positive freedom – 'freedom for.' Even if you have to live a life of poverty, you will be happy, you will be cheerful. Even if you have to chop wood to remain a poet, you will be utterly blissful, fulfilled, because you are doing what you wanted to do, you are doing your own thing. This is positive freedom.

And then there is a third freedom, the highest; in the East we have called it *moksha* – the ultimate freedom, which goes beyond both the negative and the positive. First learn saying no, then learn saying yes, and then just forget both, just be. The third freedom is not freedom against something, not for something, but just freedom. One is simply free – no question of going against, no question of going for.

'Freedom from' is political, hence all political revolutions fail – when they succeed. If they don't succeed they can go on hoping, but the moment they succeed they fail, because then they don't know what to do. That happened in the French Revolution, that happened in the Russian Revolution...that happens to every revolution. A political revolution is 'freedom from.' Once the Czar is gone, then you are at a loss: What to do now? Your whole life was devoted to fighting the Czar; you know only one thing, how to fight the Czar. Once the Czar is gone you are at a loss; your whole skill is useless. You will find yourself very empty.

'Freedom for' is artistic, creative, scientific.

And 'just freedom' is religious.

I teach you *moksha* – just freedom, neither for nor against, *neti neti*, neither this nor that, but pure freedom, just the fragrance of freedom. When the yes has destroyed your no, both can be thrown away. That is the ultimate in joy, in freedom, in realization.

Ordinarily, in your dictionaries, *responsibility* means duty, doing things the way you are expected to do them by your parents, by your teachers, by your priests, by your politicians, by somebody else. Your responsibility is to fulfill the demands made upon you by your elders and your society. If you act accordingly, you are a responsible person; if you act on your own – individually – then you are an irresponsible person.

The fact is that responsibility, the very word, has to be broken into two words. It means '*response* ability.' And response is possible only if you are spontaneous, here and now. Response means that your attention, your awareness, your consciousness, is totally here and now, in the present. So whatever happens, you respond with your whole being. It is not a question of being in tune with somebody else, some Holy Scripture, or some holy idiot. It simply means to be in tune with the present moment. This ability to respond is responsibility.

Life brings every day new situations. And if you are waiting to be guided by past experience, you will miss the opportunity to act responsibly, to act spontaneously. To me the greatest morality is to act spontaneously. And you will always be right, because your full awareness will be involved. More than that you cannot do. More than that existence cannot demand from you. And if you are focused totally in the present, what more can you do? You are bringing your whole energy and consciousness to solve the question, to get out of the situation. More than that is not possible. So whatever happens is right.

This whole idea of responsibility and being guided by experience is told to you by people who don't want you to be here and now. They go on giving you advice on how to act, what to do, but they don't know that life does not go according to their guidelines. Their guidance becomes misguidance in any real moment.

Don't be bothered by the past. What is past is past. And you have to be in the present. And this is the only way to be response-able. This is the only way to be adequate to the situation you are facing.

It is you in the final analysis – always you, the decisive factor – who decides what happens to you. Remember it. This is the very key. If you are unhappy, it is you. If you are not living rightly, it is you. If you are missing, it is you. The responsibility is totally yours. Don't be afraid of this responsibility.

Many people become too much afraid of the responsibility because they don't see the other side of the coin. On one side is written 'responsibility,' on another side is written 'freedom.' Responsibility means freedom. If somebody else is forcing you to be in misery, then you cannot get out of it – how can you get out of it, if somebody else is forcing you into misery? Unless the other decides not to make you miserable you can never get out of it. If it is you who are responsible for your misery, then it is for you to decide. If you are enjoying being miserable, be miserable a thousandfold – there is no problem. Enjoy! If you are not enjoying it, then drop it. Be clear-cut.

What I see is that people go on thinking that they want to be happy, but what can they do? – they are being forced to be miserable. This is absolutely absurd. Nobody is forcing anybody – nobody can force anybody to be miserable. A man who knows how to be happy becomes happy in any sort of situation. You cannot give him any situation in which he will not find something to be happy about. And there are persons who have learned the trick of being unhappy. You cannot give them any situation in which they will not find something to be unhappy about. Whatsoever you want to find, you will find. Life goes on supplying all sorts of things to you. You choose!

I have heard:

Two men were imprisoned. It was a full-moon night; both were standing near the window of their dark cell. The full moon was there. One was looking at the moon, and it was the rainy season and there was much water and mud just in front of the window. Dirty, and it was smelling and stinking.

One man continued to look at the moon, the other continued to look at the mud. The man who was looking at the mud, of course, was feeling very miserable. And the man who was looking at the moon was aflame, aglow; his face was reflecting the moon; his eyes were full of beauty. He had completely forgotten that he was imprisoned.

Both are standing at the same window, but they are choosing different things. There are people, if you take them to a rosebush they will count the thorns. They are great calculators, their mathematics is always right. And when they have counted thousands of thorns, it is simply logical that they will not be able to see the one rose flower. In fact, their inner world will say, 'How is it possible? – amidst so many thorns, how is a rose flower possible? It must be a deception, it must be illusory. Or even if it is possible, it is worthless.'

Then there are people who have never known the thorns of a rosebush – they look at the rose. And looking at the rose, feeling the rose, the beauty of it, celebrating the moment, they come to feel that even thorns are not so thornlike. 'How can they be, when they are growing on the same rosebush as the rose flower?' When their mind is focused on the rose flower, they start looking at thorns also in a different way: they start thinking that thorns are there to protect the rose flower. They are no longer ugly, they are no longer irrelevant; they are no longer 'anti' – a positive attitude arises.

It is up to you to make whatsoever you want out of your life. An enlightened consciousness makes even death beautiful. An unenlightened consciousness makes even life ugly. For an enlightened consciousness, only beauty exists – only beauty. Only bliss exists – only bliss.

So the question is not how to change ugliness into beauty, how to change pain into pleasure, how to change misery into happiness, no. The question is how to change the unconscious into conscious, the unenlightened attitude into the enlightened attitude – how to change your inner world of being, how to attain to life-affirmative values and drop life-negative values.

Awareness is
the Only Morality

Awareness means that whatsoever is happening in the moment is happening with complete consciousness; you are present there. If you are present when anger is happening, anger cannot happen. It can happen only when you are fast asleep. When you are present, immediate, transformation starts in your being, because when you are present, aware, many things are simply not possible. All that is called 'sin' is not possible if you are aware. So, in fact, there is only one sin, and that is unawareness.

The original word *sin* means *to miss*. It doesn't mean to commit something wrong; it simply means to miss, to be absent. The Hebrew root for the word *sin* means *to miss*. That exists in a few English words: misconduct, misbehavior. To miss means not to be there, doing something without being present – this is the only sin. And the only virtue is that while you are doing something, you are fully alert – what Gurdjieff calls self-remembering, what Buddha calls being rightly mindful, what Krishnamurti calls awareness. To be there! – that's all that is needed, nothing more. You need not change anything, and even if you try to change you cannot.

You have been trying to change many things in you. Have you succeeded? How many times have you decided not to be angry again? What happened to your decision?

When the moment comes you are again in the same trap: you become angry, and after the anger has gone, again you repent. It has become a vicious circle: you commit an act of anger and then you repent, then you are ready again to commit it.

Remember, even while you are repenting you are not there; that repentance is also part of 'sin.' That's why nothing happens. You go on trying and trying, and you take many decisions and you take many vows, but nothing happens – you remain the same. You are exactly the same as when you were born, not even a slight change has happened in you. Not that you have not tried, not that you have not tried enough – you have tried and tried and tried and you fail, because it is not a question of effort. More effort won't help. It is a question of being alert, not of making effort.

Bring a little more awareness to your existence. Each act has to be done less automatically than you have been doing up to now, and you have the key. If you are walking, don't walk like a robot. Don't go on walking as you have always walked, don't do it mechanically. Bring a little awareness to it, slow down, let each step be taken in full consciousness.

Buddha used to say to his disciples that when you raise your left foot, deep down say 'Left.' When you raise your right foot, deep down say 'Right.' First say it, so that you can become acquainted with this new process. Then slowly, slowly let the words disappear; just remember 'Left, right, left, right.'

Try it in small acts. You are not supposed to do big things. Eating, taking a bath, swimming, walking, talking, listening, cooking your food, washing your clothes – de-automatize the processes. Remember the word *de-automatization*; that is the whole secret of becoming aware.

The mind is a robot. The robot has its utility; this is the way the mind functions. You learn something; when you learn it, in the beginning you are aware. For example, if you learn swimming you are very alert, because life is in danger. Or if you learn to drive a car you are very alert. You have to be alert. You have to be careful about many things – the steering wheel, the road, the people passing by, the accelerator, the brake, the clutch. You have to be aware of everything. There are so many things to remember, and you are nervous, and it is dangerous to commit a mistake. It is so dangerous, that's why you have to keep aware. But the moment you have learned driving, this awareness will not be needed. Then the robot part of your mind will take it over.

That's what we call learning. Learning something

means it has been transferred from consciousness to the robot. That's what learning is all about. Once you have learned a thing it is no more part of the conscious, it has been delivered to the unconscious. Now the unconscious can do it; now your consciousness is free to learn something else.

This is in itself tremendously significant. Otherwise you will remain learning a single thing your whole life. The mind is a great servant, a great computer. Use it, but remember that it should not overpower you. Remember that you should remain capable of being aware, that it should not possess you *in toto*, that it should not become all and all, that a door should be left open from where you can come out of the robot.

That opening of the door is called meditation. But remember, the robot is so skillful it can even take meditation into its control. Once you have learned it, the mind says, 'Now you need not be worried about it, I am capable of doing it. I will do it, you leave it to me.'

And the mind is skillful; it is a very beautiful machine, it functions well. In fact, all our science, together with all our so-called progress in knowledge, has not yet been able to create something so sophisticated as the human mind. The greatest computers in existence are still rudimentary compared to the mind.

The mind is simply a miracle. But when something is so powerful, there is danger in it. You can be hypnotized so much by it and its power that you can lose your soul. If you have completely forgotten how to be aware, then the ego is created. Ego is the state of utter unawareness. The mind has taken possession of your whole being; it has spread like a cancer all over you, nothing is left out. The ego is the cancer of the inner, the cancer of the soul.

And the only remedy, the only remedy I say, is meditation. Then you start reclaiming a few territories from the mind. And the process is difficult but exhilarating, the process is difficult but enchanting, the process is difficult but challenging, thrilling. It will bring a new joy into your life. When you reclaim territory back from the robot you will be surprised that you are becoming a totally new person, that your being is renewed, that this is a new birth.

And you will be surprised that your eyes see more, your ears hear more, your hands touch more, your body feels more, your heart loves more – everything becomes more. And more not only in the sense of quantity, but in the sense of quality, too. You not only see more trees, you see trees more deeply. The green of the trees becomes greener – not only that, but it becomes luminous. Not only that, but the tree starts having an individuality of its own. Not only that, but you can have a communion with existence now.

And the more territories that are reclaimed, the more and more your life becomes psychedelic and colorful. You are then a rainbow – the whole spectrum; all the notes of music – the whole octave. Your life becomes richer, multi-dimensional, has depth, has height, has tremendously beautiful valleys and has tremendously beautiful sunlit peaks. You start expanding. As you reclaim parts from the robot, you start coming alive. For the first time you are turned on.

This is the miracle of meditation; this is something not to be missed.

You can be happy only if you become yourself. Nothing can be done about it, that is how it is. You can be happy only if you are yourself – but it is very difficult to find out now who you are because you have been so confused, you have been so crippled. And society has entered so deep down in you that it has become your conscience. Now your parents may be dead, your teachers may be dead – or even if they are alive they are no longer sitting on your head – but still whatsoever they have taught you goes on speaking in subtle whisperings within you.

It has become your conscience. The parental voice has

become your ego. If you do something against it, it immediately condemns you. If you do something accordingly, it applauds you, appreciates you. Still you go on being dominated by the dead.

I have heard:

Rothstein owed a hundred dollars to Wiener. The debt was past due and Rothstein was broke, so he borrowed the hundred dollars from Spevak and paid Wiener. A week later Rothstein borrowed back the hundred dollars from Wiener and paid Spevak. Another week went by and Rothstein borrowed back the hundred dollars from Spevak to pay back Wiener. He repeated this transaction several times until finally he called them up and said.

'Fellers, this is a lot of bother. Why don't you two exchange the hundred dollars every week and keep me out of it!'

This is how it has happened. First your mother, your father, your teachers, your priests – they have put things in your mind. Then one day they come and they say, 'Now you be on your own. Keep us out.' Now the conscience goes on functioning as a subtle agent.

Remember, the conscience is your bondage. A real man is conscious but he has no conscience. An unreal man is unconscious and has a very strong conscience. Conscience is given by others to you; consciousness has to be attained by you. Consciousness is your earned being, your earned quality of awareness. Conscience is given by others who wanted to manipulate you in their own ways. They had their own ideas and they manipulated you, they coerced you, tortured you into certain directions. They may not have been aware of it themselves because they were tortured by their parents.

This is how the future is dominated by the past and the present is dominated by the dead.

A real man has to drop his conscience. The parental voice has to be dropped.

There are a few sayings of Jesus, which are very rude but true to the very core. He says, 'Unless you hate your father and mother you will not be able to follow me.' Now this looks very rude. The language is rude but what he means is what I am saying to you – drop the conscience. He is not saying you should hate your father and mother, he is saying you should hate the mother's and father's voice inside you. Unless you drop that you will never be free; you will remain split, you will have many voices in you, you will never become one.

The mind is always either in the past or in the future. It cannot be in the present, it is absolutely impossible for the mind to be in the present. When you are in the present, the mind is there no more – because mind means thinking. How can you think in the present? You can think about the past; it has already become part of the memory, the mind can work it out. You can think about the future; it is not yet there, the mind can dream about it. Mind can do two things: either it can move into the past... there is space enough to move, the vast space of the past, you can go on and on and on. Or the mind can move into the future – again vast space, no end to it, you can imagine and imagine and dream. But how can mind function in the present? It has no space for the mind to make any movement.

The present is just a dividing line, that's all. It has no space. It divides the past and the future, just a dividing line. You can *be* in the present but you cannot think; for thinking, space is needed. Thoughts need space, they are just like things – remember it. Thoughts are subtle things, they are material; thoughts are not spiritual, because the dimension of the spiritual starts only when there are no thoughts. Thoughts are material things, very subtle, and every material thing needs space. You cannot be thinking in the present; the moment you start thinking it is already the past.

You see the sun is rising; you see it and you say, 'What a beautiful sunrise!' – it is already the past. When the sun is rising there is not even space enough to say, 'How beautiful!' because when you posit these two words 'How beautiful!' the experience has already become past, the mind already knows it in the memory. But exactly when the sun is rising, exactly when the sun is on the rise, how can you think? What can you think? You can *be* with the rising sun, but you cannot think. For *you* there is enough space, but not for thoughts.

A beautiful flower in the garden and you say, 'A beautiful rose' – now you are not with this rose this moment; it is already a memory. When the flower is there and you are there, both present to each other, how can you think? What can you think? How is thinking possible? There is no space for it. The space is so narrow – in fact there is no space at all – that you and the flower cannot even exist as two because there is not enough space for two, only one can exist.

That's why in a deep presence you are the flower and the flower has become you. You are also a thought – the flower is also a thought in the mind. When there is no thinking, who is the flower and who is the one who is observing? The observer becomes the observed. Suddenly boundaries are lost. Suddenly you have penetrated,

penetrated into the flower and the flower has penetrated into you. Suddenly you are not two – one exists.

If you start thinking, you have become two again. If you don't think, where is the duality? When you exist with the flower, not thinking, it is a dialogue, not a duologue but a dialogue. When you exist with your lover it is a dialogue, not a duologue, because the two are not there. Sitting by the side of your lover, holding the hand of your beloved, you simply exist. You don't think of the days past, gone; you don't think of the future reaching, coming – you are here, now. And it is so beautiful to be here and now, and so intense; no thought can penetrate this intensity. And narrow is the gate, narrow is the gate of the present. Not even two can enter into it together, only one. In the present, thinking is not possible, dreaming is not possible, because dreaming is nothing but thinking in pictures. Both are things, both are material.

When you are in the present without thinking, you are for the first time spiritual. A new dimension opens – that dimension is awareness.

No scripture can decide what is right and what is wrong. Each moment the situation changes, and each moment you have to come up with a fresh decision, whether it is right or wrong. No dead principles can help, but only living consciousness. And there is no need....

Only a blind man asks, 'Where is the door?' and, 'Should I go to the right or to the left?' But when you have eyes there is no need to ask, 'Where is the door?' – you can see. In fact, there is no need even to think where the door is; when you want to get out you simply get out, you have eyes.

Consciousness gives you eyes.

Conscience gives you only words.

Fathers and mothers go on forcing on children the idea that, 'this is your responsibility.' They have given the word responsibility a strange turn.

It simply means response-ability. Break it in two: not responsibility, but response-ability, your ability to respond. That means you have to drop all your conscience, things that people have told you are right and wrong. It may have been right and wrong for them, you have nothing to do with that.

Drop your conscience, which is imposed, and become conscious of every situation that faces you. And every moment there is a situation that faces you; become conscious of it, and out of that consciousness, act.

Whatever you do out of consciousness is right. And whatever you do unconsciously is wrong.

So to me, the act itself is not right or wrong. To me it depends on you – your consciousness, the quality of awareness that you bring to the act. Then everything has a different perspective. Consciousness is the only magic there is.

Don't be bothered about others – their problem is their problem. Don't judge them; it is none of your business. But for yourself, what is the criterion?

I am asked again and again not to criticize any religion. But they have given you ideas to judge others, fixed ideas, and life is never fixed. They have never told you how they have come upon the conclusion that something is wrong and something is right. Just their forefathers have given them the ideas.

I don't say what is right and what is wrong, I give you the criterion so whatever the situation, whatever the context, you will be always able to judge in that particular context and situation what is right and what is wrong. And such a simple thing has been missed for thousands of years. Perhaps because it is so simple and obvious, that's why it has been missed. All these so-called great thinkers and philosophers and theologians are stargazers. They don't see that which is close; their eyes are fixed far away on an imaginary God, a paradise beyond death.

I don't care at all about your gods, and I don't care at all what happens to you after your death. My concern is what happens to you right now, to your consciousness. Because that will always be with you, beyond death, wherever you are. Your consciousness will carry that light which divides the wrong from the right.

Anything that makes you more alert, more conscious, more peaceful, more silent, more celebrating, more festive, is good.

Anything that makes you unconscious, miserable, jealous, angry, destructive, is wrong.

I am not giving you a list of objects that are right and which are wrong. I am simply giving you a clarity to judge in each moment of life, without any consultation of ten commandments, of *Srimad Bhagavadgita*, without asking the dead.

Why not ask the living source of being in you?

You are the only holy scripture in the world.

And unless you are clear about this simple and obvious thing... you try. Each moment brings the opportunity. And you will see that your criterion is always helpful, and without any dictation from the dead. It is your own understanding that simply goes on shifting.

Don't listen to anybody except your own consciousness.

When you are angry, you lose consciousness, you become unconscious. Anger covers you like a black cloud. You can commit murder, you can destroy life. But when you are loving, bells of joy start ringing in your heart. You start feeling your consciousness rising. And if in love also you lose consciousness, become unconscious, then remember: you are calling lust, love. And this kind of love is not the right thing, because it is not going to help you to grow, to expand, to attain the fulfillment of your potential.

Anything that helps you to attain the fulfillment of your potential is good. It is not only a blessing to you, it is a blessing to the whole existence. No man is an island. We are all a vast, infinite continent, joined together in the roots. Maybe our branches are separate, but our roots are one.

Realizing one's potential is the only morality there is. Losing one's potential and falling into darkness and retardedness is the only sin, the only evil.

Being Total
is Being Whole

Man is split. Schizophrenia is a normal condition of man – at least now. It may not have been so in the primitive world, but centuries of conditioning, civilization, culture and religion have made man a crowd – divided, split, contradictory. One part goes one way, the other part goes in just the diametrically opposite way and it is almost impossible to keep oneself together. It is a miracle that man is existing at all. He should by now have disappeared long before. But because this split is against his nature, deep down somewhere hidden the unity still survives. Because the soul of man is one, all the conditionings at the most destroy the periphery of the man. But the center remains untouched – that's how man continues to live. But his life has become a hell.

The whole effort of Zen is in how to drop this schizophrenia, how to drop this split personality, how to drop the divided mind of man, how to become undivided, integrated, centered, crystallized.

The way you are, you cannot say that you are. You don't have a being. You are a marketplace – many voices. If you want to say yes, immediately the 'no' is there. You cannot even utter a simple word 'yes' with totality. Watch... say yes, and deep inside the 'no' also arises with it. You cannot say a simple word like 'no' without contradicting it at the same time.

In this way happiness is not possible; unhappiness is a natural consequence of a split personality. Unhappiness, because you are constantly in conflict with yourself. It is not that you are fighting with the world, you are every moment fighting with yourself. How can there be peace? How can there be silence? How can you be for even a single moment at rest? Not for a single moment are you at rest. Even while you are sleeping you are dreaming a thousand and one things. Even while sleeping you are tossing this way and that – a continuous conflict. You are a battlefield.

You say to somebody 'I love you,' and the more you say it, the more you have to repeat it. It appears there is suspicion behind it. If you really love there is no need even to say it, because words do not matter. Your whole being will show your love; your eyes will show your love. There will be no need to say it, there will be no need to repeat it continuously. You repeat to convince the other and at the same time to convince yourself – because deep down, jealousy, possessiveness, hatred, the urge to dominate, a deep power politics, are hidden.

In his epistles St. Paul uses 'in Christ' one hundred and sixty-four times. He must have been a little doubtful about it. 'In Christ… in Christ… in Christ…' one hundred and sixty-four times! It is too much. Once would have been enough. Even once is more than enough. It should be your being that shows you live in Christ – and then there is no need to say it.

Watch. Whenever you repeat a thing too many times, go deep within yourself. You must be carrying something. But you cannot falsify it, that is the problem. Your eyes will show that it is hidden behind.

Have you watched? You go to somebody's house and he welcomes you. But there is no welcome in his presence. He says, 'I am very happy to see you, glad to see you.' But you don't see any gladness anywhere; in fact, he looks a little anxious, worried, apprehensive. He looks at you as if trouble has come to his home. Have you watched people saying to you 'take any seat' and simultaneously showing you a certain seat to take? They say 'take any seat' but they show you, in a subtle gesture, 'take this seat.' They go on contradicting themselves.

Parents go on telling their children, 'Be yourself,' and at the same time they go on teaching how one should be. 'Be independent' – and at the same time they go on forcing the child to be obedient. They have their own idea about how the child should be and when they say, 'Be yourself,' they mean, 'Be the way we want you to be.' They don't mean, 'Be yourself.'

Continuously something else is there, present, and you

cannot really falsify it. But man has become cunning about that also. We don't look into each other's eyes because eyes can show the truth, so it is thought to be part of etiquette to avoid eyes. Don't look into somebody's eyes too much or you will be thought a little uncultured – transgressing, trespassing. It is very difficult to falsify the eyes. You can falsify the tongue very easily, because the tongue, the language, is a social by-product. But eyes belong to your being. You say something but your eyes continually show something else, hence in all the societies of the world people avoid each other's eyes. They don't encounter – because that will be looking into the truth.

But you can watch these contradictions in yourself and it will be a great help. Because unless your 'in' is just like your 'out' and your 'out' is just like your 'in,' you can never be at rest. In Tibet, in Egypt, they say, 'As above, so below.' Zen says, 'As within, so without.'

Unless your within becomes as your without, you can never be at rest because your periphery will continuously be in conflict with your center. The problem is that the periphery cannot win. Ultimately, only the center can win. But the periphery can delay, postpone; the periphery can waste time and life and energy. If you go on living on the periphery and just go on pretending, not really living, you will have many faces but you will not have your original face.

Mulla Nasruddin had been pulled from the river in what the police decided was a suicide attempt. When they were questioning him at headquarters he admitted that he had tried to kill himself. This is the story he told:

'Yes, I tried to kill myself. The world is against me and I wanted to end it all. I was determined not to do a half-way job so I bought a piece of rope, some matches, some kerosene and a pistol. Just in case none of those worked I went down by the river. I threw the rope over a limb hanging out over the river, I tied the rope around my neck, poured kerosene all over myself and lit the match. I jumped off the bank, put the pistol to my head and pulled the trigger.

'Guess what happened! I missed. The bullet hit the rope before I could hang myself so I fell into the river and the water put out the fire before I could burn myself. And you know, if I had not been a good swimmer, I would have ended up drowning my fool self!'

That's how things go.... You want to do a thing and yet you don't want to do it. You go on and yet you don't want to go. You live and yet you don't want to live. You even try to commit suicide and yet you don't want to commit suicide. That's why out of ten suicide attempts only one succeeds. And that too seems to be by some error. Nine attempts fail.

People are contradictory. They just don't know how to do a thing totally. And it is natural. It can be understood that when they try to commit suicide they cannot be total, because they have never been total in their lives. They don't know what totality is. They have never done a single act with their total being. Whenever an act is total, it liberates; whenever it is half-hearted it simply creates a conflict. It dissipates energy, it is destructive, it creates bondage.

In India you have heard the word *karma* – the very cause of all bondage. A karma is a karma only if it is half-hearted – then it binds you. If it is total it never binds you, then there is no bondage for you. Any act lived totally is finished. You transcend it, you never look back. Any moment lived totally leaves no trace on you – you remain unscratched, untouched by it. Your memory remains clean, you don't carry a psychological memory about it. There is no wound.

If you have loved a woman totally and she dies, there is no wound left. But if you have not loved her totally and she dies then she continues to live in the memory. Then you weep for her, you cry for her, because now you repent. There was time, there was opportunity when you could have loved her, but you could not love her. And now there is no opportunity; now she is there no more. Now there is no way to fulfill your love.

Nobody weeps and cries for somebody's death – you cry and weep for the lost opportunity to love. Your mother dies. If you have loved her really, totally, then death is beautiful, there is nothing wrong in it. You go and say goodbye to her and you don't carry any wound. You may be a little sad – naturally, she has occupied your heart for so long and now she will not be there – but that is just a passing mood. You don't carry a wound, you don't go on crying continuously, you don't hang with the past. You did whatsoever you could – you loved her, you respected her – now it is finished. One understands the helplessness of life. You are also going to be finished one day. Death is natural; one accepts it.

If you cannot accept death that simply shows there has been a contradiction in your life. You loved and yet you were withholding yourself. Now that withholding creates the problem.

If you have enjoyed your food, you forget all about it. Once you are finished, you are finished. You don't go on thinking about it. But if you were eating and you were not eating totally, if you were thinking about a thousand and one other things and you were not at the dining table at all

– you were just physically there but psychologically you were somewhere else – then you will think about food. Then food will become an obsession.

That's how sex has become an obsession in the West. Making love to a woman or to a man you are somewhere else. It is not a total act, it is not orgasmic, you are not lost in it, so a greed arises. You try to satisfy that greed, that unfulfilled desire, in a thousand ways: pornography, blue movies, and fantasy, your private movie. You go on fantasizing about women. When a real woman is there and she is ready to love you, you are not there. And when the woman is not there, you have a woman in your fantasy.

This is a very sad state of affairs. When you are eating, you are not there and then you are thinking about food, fantasizing about it. This is happening because you are not total in your act, you are always divided. While making love you are thinking of *brahmacharya*, celibacy. Then while being a celibate you are thinking of making love. You are never in tune, never in harmony.

And one goes on pretending that everything is okay so one never faces the problem.

I have heard about one couple who was known all over Poland as the most ideal couple ever. Sixty years of married life and never had there been a conflict. The wife was never known to nag the husband, the husband was never known to be rude to the wife. They had lived very peacefully – at least it appeared so.

They were celebrating their sixtieth wedding anniversary. A journalist came to interview them.

'How old is your wife?' inquired the journalist.

'She is eighty-seven,' said the husband, 'and God willing, she will live to be a hundred.'

'And how old are you?' inquired the journalist.

'Eighty-seven too,' answered the husband, 'and God willing, I will live to be a hundred and one.'

'But why,' asked the journalist, 'would you like to live a year longer than your wife?'

'To tell the truth,' said the old octogenarian, 'I would like to have at least one year of peace.'

Appearances are very deceptive. Appearances may give you respectability but they cannot give you contentment. And some day or other, in some way or other, the truth has a way of surfacing.

Truth cannot be repressed forever. If it can be repressed forever, eternally, then it is not truth. In the very definition of truth one should include the fact that truth has a way of bubbling up. You cannot go on avoiding it forever and ever. One day or other, knowingly or unknowingly, it surfaces, it reveals itself.

Truth is that which reveals itself. And just the opposite

are lies. You cannot make a lie appear as truth forever and ever. One day or other the truth will surface and the lie will be there, condemned.

You cannot avoid truth. It is better to face it, it is better to accept it, it is better to live it. Once you start living the life of truth, authenticity – of your original face – all troubles by and by disappear because the conflict drops and you are no longer divided. Your voice has a unity then, your whole being becomes an orchestra.

Many times people come to me and I ask them, 'How are you?' And they say, 'We are very, very happy.' And I cannot believe it because their faces are so dull – no joy, no delight! Their eyes have no shining in them, no light. And when they say, 'We are happy,' even the word 'happy' does not sound very happy. It sounds as if they are dragging it. Their tone, their voice, their face, the way they are sitting or standing – everything belies it, says something else. Start watching people. When they say that they are happy, watch. Watch for a clue. Are they really happy? And immediately you will be aware that something else is saying something else.

And then by and by watch yourself. When you are

saying that you are happy and you are not, there will be a disturbance in your breathing. Your breathing cannot be natural. It is impossible. Because the truth was that you were not happy. If you had said, 'I am unhappy,' your breathing would have remained natural. There was no conflict. But you said, 'I am happy.' Immediately you are repressing something – something that was coming up, you have forced down. In this very effort your breathing changes its rhythm; it is no longer rhythmical. Your face is no longer graceful, your eyes become cunning.

First watch others because it will be easier to watch others. You can be more objective about them. And when you have found clues about them use the same clues about yourself. And see – when you speak truth, your voice has a musical tone to it; when you speak untruth, something is there like a jarring note. When you speak truth you are one, together; when you speak untruth you are not together, a conflict has arisen.

Watch these subtle phenomena, because they are the consequence of togetherness or untogetherness. Whenever you are together, not falling apart; whenever you are one, in unison, suddenly you will see you are happy. That is the meaning of the word *yoga*. That's what we mean by a yogi: one who is together, in unison; whose parts are all inter-related and not contradictory, interdependent, not in conflict, at rest with each other. A great friendship exists within his being. He is whole.

Sometimes it happens that you become one, in some rare moment. Watch the ocean, the tremendous wildness of it – and suddenly you forget your split, your schizophrenia; you relax. Or, moving in the Himalayas, seeing the virgin snow on the Himalayan peaks, suddenly a coolness surrounds you and you need not be false because there is no other human being to be false to. You fall together. Or, listening to beautiful music, you fall together.

Whenever, in whatever situation you become one, a peace, a happiness, a bliss, surrounds you, arises in you. You feel fulfilled.

There is no need to wait for these moments – these moments can become your natural life. These extraordinary moments can become ordinary moments – that is the whole effort of Zen. You can live an extraordinary life in a very ordinary life: cutting wood, chopping wood, carrying water from the well, you can be tremendously at ease with yourself. Cleaning the floor, cooking food, washing the clothes, you can be perfectly at ease – because the whole question is of you doing your action totally, enjoying, delighting in it.

Life can be lived in two ways – either as calculation or as poetry. Man has two sides to his inner being: the calculative side that creates science, business, politics; and the noncalculative side, which creates poetry, sculpture, music. These two sides have not yet been bridged, they have separate existences. Because of this man is immensely impoverished, remains unnecessarily lopsided – they have to be bridged.

In scientific language it is said that your brain has two hemispheres. The left-side hemisphere calculates, is mathematical, is prose; and the right-side hemisphere of the brain is poetry, is love, is song. One side is logic, the other side is love. One side is syllogism, the other side is song. And they are not really bridged, hence man lives in a kind of split.

My effort is to bridge these two hemispheres. Man should be as scientific as possible, as far as the objective world is concerned, and as musical as possible as far as the world of relationship is concerned.

There are two worlds outside you. One is the world of objects: the house, the money, the furniture. The other is the world of persons: the wife, the husband, the mother, the children, the friend. With objects be scientific; never be scientific with persons. If you are scientific with persons you reduce them to objects, and that is one of the greatest crimes one can commit. If you treat your wife only as an object, as a sexual object, then you are behaving in a very ugly way. If you treat your husband only as a financial support, as a means, then this is immoral, then this relationship is immoral – it is prostitution, pure prostitution and nothing else.

Don't treat persons as a means, they are ends unto themselves. Relate to them – in love, in respect. Never possess them and never be possessed by them. Don't be dependent on them and don't make persons around you dependent. Don't create dependence in any way; remain independent and let them remain independent.

This is music. This dimension I call the dimension of music. And if you can be as scientific as possible with objects, your life will be rich, affluent. If you can be as musical as possible, your life will have beauty. And there is a third dimension also, which is beyond the mind – these two belong to the mind: the scientist and the artist. There is a third dimension, invisible – the dimension of no-mind. That belongs to the mystic. That is available through meditation.

Hence, these three words have to be remembered – three Ms like three Rs: mathematics, the lowest; music, just in the middle; and meditation, the highest. A perfect human being is scientific about objects, is aesthetic, musical, poetic about persons, and is meditative about himself. Where all these three meet, great rejoicing happens.

This is the real trinity, *trimurti*. In India, we worship the places where three rivers meet – we call it a *sangham*, the meeting place. And the greatest of all of them is Preyag, where the Ganges and Jamuna and Saraswati meet. Now, you can see the Ganges and you can see Jamuna, but Saraswati is invisible – you cannot see it. It is a metaphor! It simply represents, symbolically, the inner meeting of the three. You can see mathematics, you can see music, but you cannot see meditation. You can see the scientist, his work is outside. You can see the artist, his work is also outside. But you cannot see the mystic, his work is subjective. That is Saraswati – the invisible river.

You can become a sacred place, you can hallow this body and this earth; this very body the Buddha, this very earth the Lotus Paradise. This is the ultimate synthesis of all that God is.

God is known only when you have come to this synthesis; otherwise, you can believe in God, but you will not know. And belief is just hiding your ignorance. Knowing is transforming, only knowledge brings under-standing. And knowledge is not information: knowledge is the synthesis, integration, of all your potential.

Where the scientist and the poet and the mystic meet and become one – when this great synthesis happens, when all the three faces of God are expressed in you – YOU become a god. Then you can declare, '*Aham Brahmasmi!* – I am God!' Then you can say to the winds and the moon and to the rains and to the sun, '*Ana'l Haq!* – I am the truth!' Before that, you are only a seed.

When this synthesis happens, you have bloomed, blossomed – you have become the one-thousand-petaled lotus, the golden lotus, the eternal lotus, that never dies: *Aes Dhammo Sanantano*. This is the inexhaustible law that all the Buddhas have been teaching down the ages.

This is the reason why man is not meditative: The whole society forces him to be in a state of mind, not in a state of meditation.

Just imagine a world where people are meditative. It will be a simple world, but it will be tremendously beautiful. It will be silent. It will not have crimes, it will not have courts, it will not have any kind of politics. It will be a loving brotherhood, a vast commune of people who are absolutely satisfied with themselves, utterly contented with themselves. Even Alexander the Great cannot give them a gift.

If you are running to get something outside yourself, you have to be subservient to the mind. If you drop all ambitions and you are concerned more about your inner flowering, if you are more concerned about your inner juice so that it can flow and reach to others, more concerned about love, compassion, peace... then man will be meditative.

And don't be worried about making it a great movement, because this is how the mind is very tricky. You will forget all about your meditation and you will be concerned about the movement, how to make it big, how to make it world-wide, how to make many more people meditate – 'If they are not willing then force them to meditate.' It has been done; the whole of history is the proof.

Whenever you will be thinking of meditation, the mind will change the subject in such a way that you will not even be aware that the subject has been changed. The mind will start making a great movement of meditation, transforming the whole world and forgetting meditation itself. Because where is the time? – you are in a great revolution, changing the whole world.

In fact, the mind is so cunning that it condemns those people who meditate. It says, 'They are selfish, just concerned about themselves. And the whole world is dying! People need peace, and people are in tension;

people are living in hell and you are sitting silently in meditation. This is sheer selfishness.'

Mind is very cunning. You have to be very aware of it. Tell the mind, 'Don't change the subject. First I have to meditate, because I cannot share that which I don't have. I cannot share meditation with people, I cannot share love with people, I cannot share my joy with people, because I don't have it. I am a beggar; I can only pretend to be an emperor.'

But that pretension cannot last for a long time. Soon people start seeing that 'This man is just a hypocrite. He himself is tense, he himself is worried; he himself lives in pain and suffering and misery, and he is talking about creating the world as a paradise.'

So I would like to say to you: forget about it. It is your mind, which is trying to change the subject. First the meditation, and then out of it the fragrance will come, out of it the light will come. Out of it, words which are not dead but alive, words which have authority in them will come. And they may help others, but that is not going to be your goal; it will be a byproduct.

The changing of other people through meditation is a byproduct, it is not a goal. You become a light unto yourself, and that will create the urge to become a light to many people who are thirsty. You become the example, and that example will bring the movement on its own accord.

In the search of one's own self there is always a danger that you may choose the inner against the outer – then the withdrawal becomes schizoid, because you become lopsided, you lose balance.

Balance is health. To lose balance is to lose health. And balance is sanity – to lose balance is to become insane. The fear is always there. The danger is always there. The danger comes because of your mind.

It is always easy for the mind to change its diseases. Somebody is mad after women; only sex is his obsession. One day or other he will be fed up with this, tired of it all. He will start moving to the other extreme: he will start thinking of celibacy, of becoming a Catholic monk or something.

There is danger. It is as if you have been eating too much and then one day you decide to fast. Eating too much is bad but fasting is not better. In fact, by eating too much you are not going to die so soon; you may become heavier, fatty, uglier, but you will linger on, you will drag on. But by fasting, within weeks you will disappear; you cannot survive more than three months. Both are dangerous.

Eating too much is neurotic. Fasting is the opposite

neurosis, but still neurotic. Have a balanced diet. Eat as much as is needed by the body; don't go on stuffing your body. But this is how it happens. I have been watching people: whenever a society becomes very rich, fasting comes as a cult. In India, Jains are one of the richest societies – fasting is their cult, fasting is their religion. When America became very rich, fasting started to become more and more a fashion. It was difficult to find a woman who was not on a diet. People went to nature cure clinics to fast.

A poor man's religion is always of festivity, feast. Mohammedans, who are mostly poor people in India, when their religious day comes they feast. They starve the whole year so, of course on the religious day, at least on that day, they change their clothes – new clothes, colorful – and they enjoy. At least for one day they can enjoy. Jains feast the whole year, and when their religious days come they fast. That is logical. A poor man's festival is going to be a feast; a rich man's festival is going to be a fast. People move to the opposite extreme.

So when you start meditating, there is a danger that you may become too much attached to this introversion. Meditation is an introversion; it leads you to your center. If you lose your elasticity and you become incapable of coming back to the periphery, then it is a withdrawal – and a dangerous withdrawal. It is schizoid.

Be alert! That has happened to many people. The whole history is full of such people who became schizoid.

When you are meditating, always remember that the periphery is not to be lost permanently. You have to come to the periphery again and again so the route remains clear and the path remains there. Hence my insistence to meditate but not to renounce the world. Meditate in the morning and then go to the market; meditate in the morning and then go to your office. Meditate and then make love! Don't create any dichotomy, don't create any conflict. Don't say, 'Now how can I love? I am a meditator.' Then you are moving in a dangerous direction; sooner or later you will lose all contact with the periphery. Then you will become frozen at the center. And life consists of being alive – changing, moving. Life is dynamic, it is not dead.

There are two types of dead people in the world: dead on the periphery and dead on the center. Become the third type: alive in between; go on moving from the center to the periphery, from the periphery to the center. They are enriching to each other; they are enhancing to each other. Just watch! If you meditate and then make love, your love will have a tremendously new depth to it. Love and then meditate and suddenly you will see: when your energy is full of love, meditation goes so deep and so easily. You simply ride on the wave – you need not make any effort. You simply float and reach higher and higher and higher. Once you understand the rhythm of the polar opposites, then there is no fear.

Remember: life is a rhythm between day and night, summer and winter. It is a continuous rhythm. Never stop anywhere! Be moving! And the bigger the swing, the deeper your experience will be.

From Relationship
to Relating

Love is not a relationship. Love relates, but it is not a relationship. A relationship is something finished. A relationship is a noun; the full stop has come, the honeymoon is over. Now there is no joy, no enthusiasm, now all is finished. You can carry it on, just to keep your promises. You can carry it on because it is comfortable, convenient, cozy. You can carry it on because there is nothing else to do. You can carry it on because if you disrupt it, it is going to create much trouble for you.

Relationship means something complete, finished, closed. Love is never a relationship; love is relating. It is always a river, flowing, unending. Love knows no full stop; the honeymoon begins but never ends. It is not like a novel that starts at a certain point and ends at a certain point. It is an ongoing phenomenon. Lovers end, love continues. It is a continuum. It is a verb, not a noun. And why do we reduce the beauty of relating to relationship? Why are we in such a hurry? – because to relate is insecure, and relationship is a security. Relationship has a certainty – relating is just a meeting of two strangers, maybe just an overnight stay and in the morning we say goodbye. Who knows what is going to happen tomorrow? And we are so afraid that we want to make it certain, we want to make it predictable. We would like tomorrow to be according to our ideas; we don't allow it freedom to have its own say. So we immediately reduce every verb to a noun.

You are in love with a woman or a man and immediately you start thinking of getting married. Make it a legal contract. Why? How does the law come into love? The law comes into love because love is not there. It is only a fantasy, and you know the fantasy will disappear. Before it disappears settle down, before it disappears do something so it becomes impossible to separate.

In a better world, with more meditative people, with a little more enlightenment spread over the earth, people will love, love immensely, but their love will remain a relating, not a relationship. And I am not saying that their love will be only momentary. There is every possibility their love may go deeper than your love, may have a higher quality of intimacy, may have something more of poetry and more of God in it. And there is every possibility their love may last longer than your so-called relationship ever lasts. But it will not be guaranteed by the law, by the court, by the policeman.

The guarantee will be inner. It will be a commitment from the heart, it will be a silent communion. If you enjoy being with somebody, you would like to enjoy it more and more. If you enjoy the intimacy, you would like to explore the intimacy more and more.

And there are a few flowers of love which bloom only after long intimacies. There are seasonal flowers too; within six weeks they are there in the sun, but within six weeks again they are gone forever. There are flowers that take years to come, and there are flowers that take many years to come. The longer it takes, the deeper it goes.

But it has to be a commitment from one heart to another heart. It has not even to be verbalized, because to verbalize it is to profane it. It has to be a silent commitment; eye to eye, heart to heart, being to being. It has to be understood, not said.

Forget relationships and learn how to relate. Once you are in a relationship you start taking each other for granted. That's what destroys all love affairs. The woman thinks she knows the man, the man thinks he knows the woman. Nobody knows either. It is impossible to know the other, the other remains a mystery. And to take the other for granted is insulting, disrespectful.

To think that you know your wife is very, very ungrateful. How can you know the woman? How can you know the man? They are processes, they are not things. The woman that you knew yesterday is not there today. So much water has gone down the Ganges; she is somebody else, totally different. Relate again, start again, don't take it for granted.

And the man that you slept with last night, look at his face again in the morning. He is no longer the same person, so much has changed. So much, incalculably much, has changed. That is the difference between a thing and a person. The furniture in the room is the same, but the man and the woman, they are no more the same. Explore again, start again. That's what I mean by relating.

Relating means you are always starting, you are continuously trying to become acquainted. Again and again, you are introducing yourself to each other. You are trying to see the many facets of the other's personality. You are trying to penetrate deeper and deeper into his realm of inner feelings, into the deep recesses of his being. You are trying to unravel a mystery which cannot be unraveled.

That is the joy of love: the exploration of consciousness. And if you relate, and don't reduce it to a relationship, then the other will become a mirror to you. Exploring him, unawares you will be exploring yourself too. Getting deeper into the other, knowing his feelings, his thoughts, his deeper stirrings, you will be knowing your own deeper stirrings too. Lovers become mirrors to each other, and then love becomes a meditation. Relationship is ugly, relating is beautiful.

In relationship both persons become blind to each other. Just think, how long has it been since you saw your wife eye to eye? How long has it been since you looked at your husband? Maybe years. Who looks at one's own wife? You have already taken it for granted that you know her. What more is there to look at? You are more interested in strangers than in the people you know – you know the whole topography of their bodies, you know how they respond, you know everything that has happened is going to happen again and again. It is a repetitive circle.

It is not so, it is not really so. Nothing ever repeats; everything is new every day. Just your eyes become old, your assumptions become old, your mirror gathers dust and you become incapable of reflecting the other.

Hence I say relate. By saying relate, I mean remain continuously on a honeymoon. Go on searching and seeking each other, finding new ways of loving each other, finding new ways of being with each other. And each person is such an infinite mystery, inexhaustible, unfathomable, that it is not possible that you can ever say, 'I have known her,' or, 'I have known him.' At the most you can say, 'I have tried my best, but the mystery remains a mystery.'

In fact the more you know, the more mysterious the other becomes. Then love is a constant adventure.

The really aware person is one who is capable of living alone. But that is only half the truth. The other half is that the one who is really capable of being alone is also capable of being together with somebody. In fact only he is capable of being in togetherness.

The person who is not able to be alone cannot be together with somebody, because he has no individuality. The person who has no individuality cannot be together with somebody – why? There are many problems. First, he is always afraid that if he comes too close to the other person he will lose himself. He has no integrity yet: he is afraid.

That's why people are afraid of love, of too much love. People are afraid to come too close, because if they come too close they may dissolve in the other. That is the fear. The other may overpower them, the other may become their whole reality. They may be possessed by the other – that is the fear.

Only a person who knows the beauty of being alone is capable of coming as close as possible, because he is unafraid. He knows that he *is*, he has an integrated being in him. He has something crystallized in him, because without that crystallized something he would not be able to be alone.

The second thing: when a person is not capable of being alone he is always dependent on the other. He clings – because he is afraid the other may leave, and then he will have to suffer loneliness. He clings, he exploits the other, he creates all kinds of bondages around the other.

And whenever you make the other your possession, you become the possession of the other. It functions in both ways. When you reduce the other to a slave, the other reduces you to a slave. And when you are so afraid of the other's leaving you, you are ready to compromise; you are ready to compromise in any way.

You will see this happening to all husbands and wives. They have compromised, they have sold their souls, for a single reason: because they cannot be alone. They are afraid the woman may leave, the man may leave – and then? They very idea is so frightening, scary.

The capacity to be alone is the capacity to love. It may look paradoxical to you, but it is not. It is an existential truth: only those people who are capable of being alone are capable of love, of sharing, of going into the deepest core of the other person – without possessing the other, without becoming dependent on the other, without reducing the other to a thing, and without becoming addicted to the other. They allow the other absolute freedom, because they know that if the other leaves, they will be as happy as they are now. Their happiness cannot be taken by the other, because it is not given by the other.

Then why do they want to be together? It is no longer a need, it is a luxury. Try to understand it. Real persons love each other as a luxury; it is not a need. They enjoy sharing: they have so much joy, they would like to pour it into somebody. And they know how to play their life as a solo instrument.

The solo flute player knows how to enjoy his flute alone. And if he comes and finds a tabla player, a solo tabla player, they both will enjoy being together and creating a harmony between the flute and the tabla. They both will enjoy it: they will both pour their richnesses into each other.

But the society consists of people who are needful, who are all dependent in some way or other. The children are dependent on the parents – but remember, the parents are also dependent on the children. It may not be so obvious, but it is so – just search a little more. The mother cannot be without the child; of course the child cannot be without the mother, but the mother also cannot be without the child.

Family members are dependent on each other, they cling to each other. It gives a certain comfort, security, safety. Then the family depends on other families. People depend on the church, people depend on clubs, people depend on societies. It is a great world of dependent people, childish ungrownups.

A commune, in my vision, is a totally different world. It is not a society. A commune is a gathering of people who are all capable of being alone, and they would like to be together to create a great orchestra of being. A commune is not a dependent phenomenon, it is an independence.

That's why many times in my commune people come and tell me, 'Everybody here seems to be so happy with himself that it looks as if nobody is interested in anybody else.' Particularly the newcomers feel it, that it is as if people are indifferent. It is not so; they are not indifferent. But you are coming from a society where everybody is dependent on everybody else. This is not a society, not like your old society. Here everybody is enjoying his being, and nobody interferes in anybody's life; there is no interference.

My whole effort is to make you so alert, so loving, that you don't interfere. Love never interferes, love gives total freedom. If it is not giving freedom, then it is not love. It is not indifference that newcomers feel – and, slowly slowly, they understand. By the time they have lived here for a few weeks, they know what is happening. People are not indifferent, people are very loving. But they are non-interfering, so they don't impinge upon you. And they are non-needy, they are not greedy, they don't cling to you.

Of course, you have known only that kind of people, so this new type frightens you. You think that you are not needed, that nobody cares, that these people are very selfish, that they are too self-occupied. It is nothing like that; that is not the case at all, it is absolutely untrue. But to you it may appear so in the beginning.

A commune of seekers will be a celebration, a gathering of people who are not in any way needy of the other. It is beautiful if two persons are together; it is good if it continues and they can sing a song together, it is good to sing a chorus. But if things go wrong, if it becomes heavy, if being together interferes with your freedom, then you can go and sing your song alone. There is no need to be part of a chorus.

And the commune is a space where this much freedom is allowed. There will be couples, but there will not be husbands and wives. There will be *friends* in the commune.

People can live together if they enjoy being together, but only just for that joy of being together – it is not a need. If at any moment a person decides to get out of a relationship, he can get out of it without any trouble, without any turmoil, without any crying and weeping and fighting and making things ugly, without any nagging and prolonging.

People have to be true. If they feel good being together, good. If they feel it is no longer growthful, it is no longer maturing, they say goodbye to each other. They feel grateful to each other: whatsoever has been shared was beautiful, they will cherish the memory for ever, but now the time has come to depart. They lived in joy, they will depart in joy; their friendship will remain intact. And it may happen again: they may start living together again. They will not leave any scars on each other, they will not wound each other, they will respect the other's freedom.

My commune particularly – and whatsoever I am saying, I am saying about my commune – my commune will create individuals who are capable of being alone and who are also capable of being together – who can play solo music and who can become part of a chorus.

If you are alert, many things simply drop; you need not drop them. In awareness certain things are not possible. And this is my definition, there is no other criterion. You cannot 'fall in love' if you are aware; then falling in love is a sin. You can love but it will not be like a fall, it will be like a rise.

Why do we use the term 'falling in love'? It *is* a falling; you are falling, you are not rising. When you are aware, falling is not possible – not even in love! It is not possible, it is simply not possible. With awareness, it is impossible;

you *rise* in love. And rising in love is a totally different phenomenon from falling in love. Falling in love is a dream state. That's why people who are in love, you can see it from their eyes: as if they are more asleep than others, intoxicated, dreaming. You can see from their eyes because their eyes have a sleepiness. People who rise in love are totally different. You can see they are no longer in a dream, they are facing the reality and they are growing through it.

Falling in love you remain a child; rising in love you mature. And, by and by, love becomes not a relationship, it becomes a state of your being. Then it is not that you love this and you don't love that, no – you are simply love. Whosoever comes near you, you share with them. Whatsoever is happening, you give your love to it. You touch a rock, and you touch as if you are touching your beloved's body. You look at the tree, and you look as if you are looking at your beloved's face. It becomes a state of being. Not that you are 'in love' – now you *are* love. This is rising, this is not falling.

Love is beautiful when you rise through it, and love becomes dirty and ugly when you fall through it. And sooner or later you will find that it proves poisonous, it becomes a bondage. You have been caught in it, your freedom has been crushed. Your wings have been cut; now you are free no more. Falling in love you become a possession: you possess, and you allow somebody to possess you. You become a thing, and you try to convert the other person you have fallen in love with into a thing.

Look at a husband and a wife: they both have become like things, they are persons no more. Both are trying to possess each other. Only things can be possessed, persons never. How can you possess a person? How can you dominate a person? How can you convert a person into a possession? Impossible! But the husband is trying to possess the wife; the wife is trying the same. Then there is a clash, then they both become basically enemies. Then they are destructive to each other.

This is no longer love. In fact when you possess a person, you hate, you destroy, you kill; you are a murderer. Love should give freedom; love *is* freedom. Love will make the beloved more and more free, love will give wings, and love will open the vast sky. It cannot become a prison, an enclosure. But that love you don't know because that happens only when you are aware; that quality of love comes only when there is awareness. You know a love which is a sin, because it comes out of sleep.

And this is so for everything you do. Even if you try to do something good, you harm.

Doing Good, Serving Humanity, and Other Roads to Hell

Look at the do-gooders: they always do harm, they are the most mischievous people in the world. Social reformers, so-called revolutionaries, they are the most mischievous people. But it is difficult to see where their mischief lies because they are very good people, they are always doing good to others – that is their way of creating an imprisonment for the other. If you allow them to do something good to you, you will be possessed by them.

They start by massaging your feet, and sooner or later you will find their hands reach your neck! At the feet they start, at the neck they end – because they are unaware, they don't know what they are doing. They have learned a trick: that if you want to possess someone, do good. They are not even conscious that they have learned this trick. But they will do harm because anything, anything that tries to possess the other person, whatsoever its name or form, is irreligious, is a sin. Your churches, your temples, your mosques, they have all committed sins on you because they all became possessors, they all became dominations.

Every church is against religion because religiousness is freedom. Why does it happen then? Jesus tries to give freedom, wings to you. Then what happens, how does this church come in? It happens because Jesus lives on a totally different plane of being, the plane of awareness – and those who listen to him, those who follow him, they live on the plane of sleep. Whatsoever they hear, interpret, it is interpreted through their own dreams – and whatsoever they create is going to be a sin. Christ gives you religiousness and then people who are fast asleep convert it into a church.

It is said that once Satan, the devil, was sitting under a tree, very sad. A saint was passing; he looked at Satan and he said, 'We have heard that you never rest, you are always doing some mischief or other somewhere or other. What are you doing here sitting under the tree?'

Satan was really depressed. He said, 'It seems my work has been taken over by the priests, and I cannot do anything – I am completely unemployed. Sometimes I have the idea of committing suicide because these priests are doing so well.'

Priests have done so well because they converted freedom into imprisonments, they converted truth into dogmas – they converted everything from the plane of awareness to the plane of sleep.

You cannot help if you are miserable, you will only contaminate people's lives with your misery. You cannot help if you are full of darkness, you will create shadows in other people's lives. If you are stinking you cannot share your fragrance with others. What fragrance? – there is no fragrance at all. You are simply stinking! you will be sharing whatsoever you have.

If you are angry you will share anger, if you are greedy you will share greed, if you are full of lust you will share your lust. We can share only that which we have, we cannot share that which we don't have. This has to be the fundamental thing to be remembered; hence the first step is meditation and the second step is compassion.

First help yourself. I teach absolute selfishness, because this is my observation, my experience, that if you can be truly selfish, out of that true selfishness altruism is born and only out of that. There is no other way. A truly selfish person is one who tries in every possible way to be blissful, to be peaceful. The truly selfish person is one who first tries to find god for himself. His concern is absolutely selfish. He is not concerned with anybody – the poverty in the world and the ill people and the old people and this and that – he is simply concerned with one thing, his effort is one-pointed. Like an arrow he goes withinwards to find that still point from where life goes through a radical change.

Once that point is reached then it is going to be a simple phenomenon – compassion, service, help. You can help then. It will be a joy to be shared. You won't feel any ego, that you are helping people, you won't feel holierthan-thou, you will be simply rejoicing. You won't gather any kind of ego out of you compassion. The ego is already gone, it is dead. It died in your meditation, now it cannot come back. And a man without the ego can be of tremendous help. Otherwise the so-called helpers of mankind and missionaries and servants of people, they are all mischievous people. They have created more mischief in the world than anybody else. Beware!

Can you say that you are utterly contented, that you don't need even a single moment more to live because there is nothing left for you? Are you saved from all anxiety, anguish, misery, suffering, anger, jealousy? Are you saved from your own ego? If you are not saved from all this rubbish hanging around, all this poison in your being, you have some nerve to ask how to save humanity.

And who are we to save humanity? On what authority? I can never conceive myself as a savior, as a messiah, because these are all ego trips. Who am I to save you? If I can save myself, that is more than enough.

But it is a strange world. People are themselves drowning in shit, and crying loudly, 'Save humanity!'

From whom? From you?

It is psychologically understandable. You start all these ideas of redeeming, saving, helping, serving, just to do one thing: to escape from yourself. You don't want to face yourself. You don't want to see where you are, what you are. The best way is, start saving humanity so you will be so much involved, engaged, occupied, worried about great problems that your own problems will look negligible. Perhaps you may forget all about them. This is a very psychological device, but very poisonous. You want somehow to be as far away from yourself as possible so you need not see the wounds which are hurting. The best way is: serve.

I used to go to speak in Rotary Clubs, and on their desk they have their motto: We serve. And that was enough to trigger me. 'What nonsense is this? Whom do you serve and why should you serve? Who are you to serve?' But Rotarians all over the world believe in service; and once in a while they do little things, very clever.

The Rotarians collect all the medicines which are left in your house, unused because the sick person is no longer sick. Half the bottle is left – what are you going to do with it? Set up some bank account in the other world; give it to the Rotary Club! You are not losing anything, you were going to throw it out anyway. What were you going to do with that medicine, those tablets, injections, or any other things that are left? You just give it to the Rotary Club. The

Rotary Club collects all kinds of medicines from everybody, and it has all the top people of the city. It is a prestigious thing to be a member of a Rotary Club, to be a Rotarian. So the doctor who is the Rotarian will distribute those medicines to poor people. Great service! The doctor takes his fee, and finds out from this junk that they have collected what medicine may be in some way useful. He is doing great service, because at least he is giving this much time in finding the medicine from out of the junk: 'We serve.' And then he feels great inside that he is doing something of immense value.

One man had been opening schools in India for aboriginal children his whole life. He was a follower of Gandhi. Just by chance he met me, because I had gone into one of the aboriginal tribes where he was opening a school. I was studying those aboriginals from every view, because they were living examples of days when man was not so much burdened with all kinds of morality, religion, civilization, culture, etiquette, manners. They were simple, innocent, still wild, fresh.

This man was going and collecting money from cities, and opening schools and bringing teachers. Just by the way he met me there. I said, 'What are you doing? You think you are doing great service to these people?'

He said, 'Of course!'

So arrogantly he said, 'Of course!' I said, 'You are not aware of what you are doing. Schools exist in the cities, better than these: what help have they provided for human beings? And if those schools cannot provide, and colleges and universities cannot provide any help to humanity, what do you think? – your small schools are going to help these poor aboriginals? All that you will do is to destroy their originality. All that you will do is to destroy their primitive wildness. They are still free: your schools will create nothing but trouble for them.'

The man was shocked, but he waited for a few seconds and then said, 'Perhaps you are right, because once in a while I have been thinking that these schools and colleges and universities exist on a far wider scale all over the world. What can my small schools do? But it was Gandhi's wish for me to go to aboriginals and open schools, so I am following my master's order.'

I said, 'If your master was an idiot, that does not mean that you have to continue following the order. Now, stop – I order you! And I tell you why you have been doing all this – just to escape from your own suffering, your own misery. You are a miserable man; anybody can see it from your face. You have never loved anybody, you have never been loved by anybody.'

He said, 'How did you manage to infer that? – because it

is true. I was an orphan, nobody loved me, and I have been brought up in Gandhi's ashram where love was only talked about in prayer; otherwise, love was not a thing to be practiced. There was strict discipline, a kind of regimentation. So nobody has ever loved me, that's true; and you are right, I have never loved anybody because in Gandhi's ashram it was impossible to fall in love. That was the greatest crime.

'I was one of those whom Gandhi praised because I never fell in his eyes. Even his own sons betrayed him. Devadas, his son, fell in love with a woman and then he was expelled from the ashram; they got married. Gandhi's own personal secretary fell in love with a woman and kept the love affair secret for years. When it was exposed it was a scandal, a great scandal.'

This poor man was praised because he never came in contact with any woman! Gandhi sent him to the aboriginal tribes and he had been doing what his master had said. But he said to me, 'You have disturbed me. Perhaps it is true: I am just trying to escape from myself, from my wounds, from my own anguish.'

So all these people who become interested in saving humanity, in the first place are egoistic. They are thinking of themselves as saviors. In the second place, they are sick. They are trying to forget their sickness. And in the third place, whatever they do is going to help man become worse than he is, because they are sick and blind and they are trying to lead people. And when blind people lead, then you can be certain sooner or later the whole lot is going to fall into a well.

No, I am not interested in saving anybody. In fact, nobody needs saving. Everybody is perfectly okay as he is. Everybody is what he has chosen to be. Now who am I to disturb him? All that I can do is, I can say about myself what has happened to me. I can tell my story. Perhaps from that story someone may get an insight, a direction. Perhaps from that a door opens up. But I am not doing anything, I am simply sharing my own experience.

It is not service, I am enjoying it, so it is not service. Remember it. A servant has to be very long-faced and very serious – he is doing such a great work. He is carrying the Himalayas on his shoulders, the whole burden of the world. I am not carrying anything, no burden of the world, no burden of anybody, and I am not doing any serious job.

I am just enjoying telling you about my experience. To share it is a joy in itself.

The world is sad, it is in misery. There is great suffering in the hearts of people. But you need not be sad about it, for the simple reason that by becoming sad you join them, you create more sadness. It is not a help. It is just as if people are sick, and you see their sickness and you also become sick. Your sickness is not going to make them healthy, it is simply creating more sickness.

To feel for their sadness does not mean to become sad. To feel for their sadness means to look for the causes of what is creating all their suffering and misery, and to help them to remove those causes. And at the same time you have to remain as joyful as possible because your joy is going to help them, not your sadness. You have to be cheerful. They should know that there is a possibility of being cheerful in this sad world. They have completely lost hope, because everywhere they look there is sadness. They have accepted the fact that sadness is just the nature of things – you cannot do anything about it, you have to suffer it.

And the religious teachers have only been giving them consolations, giving them some hocus-pocus, hypocritical ideas. They have kept them miserable for centuries because they have made them accept misery as part of life. Not only that, they have raised their sadness and misery to some spiritual status. They have been telling them,

'Blessed are the poor.' So not only have they accepted their sadness as just a simple fact of life about which you cannot do anything, but they have also started feeling good about it, feeling it is something spiritual, that it is a test given by God to them.

Rich people are not going to enter into the kingdom of God; it will be the poor, the miserable – they will be received with great joy and welcomed. All that they have to do is not to make any fuss about their misery – accept it as a blessing in disguise. And if for centuries you go on saying such things, you poison people's minds. But it seems that they are not alone in their sadness; everybody is sad. In fact, they will feel afraid to be cheerful in this vast crowd of sad people.

So it is not going to help if when seeing them sad, you also become sad. It is simply making them more convinced of the fact that joy does not exist on the earth, it is something otherworldly – the fate and the destiny of the earth is misery. So simply give them an example that it is not true: 'If I can be cheerful, rejoicing, your whole fabric of stupid theories is proved irrelevant.'

Asleep and Awake

A little boy was playing with his blocks when his father entered the room.

'Quiet, Dad, I am building a church.'

The father, thinking that he would test his son along the lines of religious knowledge said, 'Why do we want to be quiet in church?'

'We have to, because the people are sleeping.'

Man is asleep. This sleep is not the ordinary sleep, it is a metaphysical sleep. Even while you think you are awake, you remain asleep. With open eyes, walking on the road, working in your office, you remain asleep. It is not only in the church that you are asleep, you are asleep everywhere. You are simply asleep.

This metaphysical sleep has to be broken, this metaphysical sleep has to be completely dropped. One has to become a flame of awareness. Only then does life start being meaningful, only then does life gain a significance, only then is life not the so-called day-to-day, ordinary, dull routine – life has poetry in it and a thousand and one lotuses flower in the heart. Then there is God.

God is not a theory, it is not an argument. It is an experience of significance in life. And the significance can only be felt when you are not asleep. How can you feel the significance of life in sleep? Life is significant, immensely significant. Each moment of it is precious. But you are asleep. Only awakened eyes can see this significance, live this significance.

Just the other day there was a question. Somebody asked: 'Osho, you go on telling us to celebrate life. What is there to celebrate?' I can understand. His question is relevant. There seems to be nothing to celebrate. What is there to celebrate? His question is your question, is everybody's question.

But reality is just the contrary. There is everything to celebrate. Each moment is so immense, is so fantastic, each moment brings such an ecstasy.... But you are asleep. The ecstasy comes, hovers around you and goes. The breeze comes, dances around you and goes. And you remain asleep. The flowers bloom and the fragrance comes to you, but you are asleep. God goes on singing in a thousand and one ways, God dances around you; but you are asleep.

You ask me: What is there to celebrate? What *isn't* there to celebrate? Everything that one can imagine is there. Everything that one can desire is there. And it is more than you can imagine. It is in abundance. Life is a luxury!

Just think of a blind man. He has never seen a rose

flower bloom. What has he missed? Do you know? Can't you feel any compassion for him? That he has missed something, something divine? He has not seen a rainbow. He has not seen the sunrise or the sunset. He has not seen the green foliage of the trees. He has not seen color. How dull his consciousness is! And you have eyes and you say, What is there to celebrate? The rainbow is there, the sunset is there, the green trees are there, such a colorful existence.

And yet I understand. Your question is relevant. I understand that this question has some meaning. The rainbow is there, the sunset is there, the ocean, the clouds, all are there – but you are asleep. You have never looked at the rose flower. You have passed by, you have seen the rose flower – I am not saying you have not seen it, you have eyes so you see – but you have not looked at it. You have not meditated upon it, you have not given a single moment of your meditation to it. You have never been in tune with it, you have never been by the side of it, sitting close by, in communion. You have never said 'hello' to it, you have never participated with it. Life passes by, you are just there, not participating. You are not *en rapport* with life, that's why your question is meaningful. You have eyes and yet you don't see, you have ears yet you don't hear, you have a heart yet you don't love – you are fast asleep.

This has to be understood, that's why I go on repeating

it again and again. If you understand that you are asleep, the first ray of awakening has entered you. If you can feel that you are asleep then you are no more, then you are just on the verge of where the day breaks – the morning, the dawn.

But the first essential is to understand that 'I am asleep.' If you think you are not asleep then you will never be awake. If you think that this life which you have been living up to now is a life of an awakened being, then why should you seek and search ways to awaken yourself? When a man dreams, and dreams that he is awake, why should he try to be awake? He already believes that he is awake. This is the greatest trick of the mind and everybody is befooled by this trick. The greatest trick of the mind is to give you the idea of that which you are not, and to help you feel that you are already that.

Gurdjieff used to tell a parable.... There was a magician who was also a shepherd. He had thousands of sheep to look after and he was a very miserly man so he didn't want many servants and he didn't want many watchmen. He did not want to pay anybody and he did not want his sheep to be lost or taken by the wolves. But it was very difficult for him to take care of all the sheep alone. He was very rich and he had many sheep.

So he played a trick on the sheep. He hypnotized them – he was a magician. He hypnotized them and told every sheep, 'You are not a sheep. Don't be afraid.' To some he said, 'You are a lion.' To some he said, 'You are tigers.' To some he even said, 'You are men. Nobody is going to kill you. Don't be afraid and don't try to escape from here.'

The sheep started believing in his hypnosis. Every day he would butcher a few sheep but the others would think, 'We are not sheep. He is butchering only sheep. We are lions, we are tigers, we are wolves, we are this and that...' even that they were men. Some were even told that they were magicians – and they believed it. It was always some sheep which was to be butchered. They remained aloof, distant. They were not worried. And by and by they were all butchered.

'This is the situation,' Gurdjieff used to say.

When somebody dies, has the question occurred to you that it is your death? No, the mind goes on playing the game. The mind says it is always the other that dies, it is never you.

Sometimes an old man comes to me, very old. And he is always worried about my death. He asks, 'Osho, if you die, what will happen to me?' He is nearabout seventy-five. I am always surprised when he says, 'If you die what is going to happen to me?: Osho is going to die and he is not going to die! There is every possibility he will die before me, but about that he never asks. Whenever he comes this is his question,

'Don't leave me. If you die, what will happen to me?'

This is how the mind goes on functioning. It is always somebody else who dies. Have you not seen people in their cars rushing with mad speed? Why? There is a deep idea in the mind that accidents happen to others. Even on boards it is written how many accidents are happening every day, how many people died yesterday, yet people go on rushing by. Who bothers? These things happen to others. 'These accidents, yes, they happen, but they never happen to me.' That idea persists. Gurdjieff's parable is not just a parable.

All that is wrong happens to somebody else. Even death. You cannot conceive of your own death. And if you cannot conceive of your own death, you cannot become religious. Even to think about it seems impossible – how can I die? How?

One goes on keeping oneself separate from all, one goes on believing that one is the exception. Watch out! Whenever you feel that you are the exception, remember, the mind is going to deceive you. The magician of the mind is tricking you. And it has tricked everybody. This is the metaphysical sleep. 'Death is not going to happen to me. And I am already that which I want to be. And everything is good. And I am awake. And I already know. So what is there to seek and search for?'

These false notions, these absurd ideas have been

repeated for so long that you have been hypnotized by them. You have auto-hypnotized yourself. The magician is not somewhere outside, it is your own mind. It takes all significance away from you. Significance is only in awareness, significance is awareness. It is a kind of radiance. When you become aflame with awareness everything becomes aflame with significance.

It is you who are reflected in existence – the existence functions as a mirror. If you are dull and dead, there is nothing to celebrate because existence simply shows your dull and dead face. What is there to celebrate? If you are alive, flowering, singing a song, dancing a dance, the mirror reflects a dance, a song – there is much to celebrate. When you celebrate there is much more to celebrate, and it goes on and on. There is no end to it. If you don't celebrate, by and by you become more and more dead and more and more dull. There is less and less to celebrate. One day suddenly life is absolutely meaningless.

Children are more alert than they will ever be again in their life unless they deliberately start seeking some path of awareness, some path of meditation. Unless by accident they come close to a master – a Sufi, a Zen master, a Hassid – they will get more and more into the mire of sleep. Children are born awake and old people die fast asleep, snoring. If you are asleep there is no celebration.

But why – why is man asleep? What is the root cause of it? It is a way to avoid; sleep is a way to avoid. There are many problems in life. Obviously they are there. When I say celebrate, I don't mean there are no problems. Problems are there. They have to be encountered, they have to be transcended. And celebration is a way to encounter them.

I am not saying there are no problems, I am not telling you fairy tales, I am not telling you that there are no problems and that life is simply beautiful and there are no thorns and only rose flowers – there are not. For every one rose, there exist one thousand thorns. I am not creating a dream for you, a utopia. I am utterly realistic and pragmatic.

But the way to get beyond the thorns is to celebrate life, is to celebrate that one flower. In fact, that one flower is more precious because there are one thousand thorns. If there were all flowers and flowers and no thorns, flowers would be meaningless. It is because of darkness that the morning is so beautiful, it is because of death that life has such joy, it is because of illness that health is significant.

I am not saying there is nothing to be worried about. There are many things, but there is no need to worry about them. They can be encountered. They can be encountered without any worry, they can be encountered through celebration. There are only two ways to encounter them: one is the way of worry and the other is the way of celebration. The way of worry is the way of the world; the way of celebration is the way of religion. The way of worry creates sleep – there are so many worries, how to get rid of them? You don't know. Not even a single worry can be solved.

For example, there is death. How can you solve it? What can you do to solve it? It is there, naked in front of you. You cannot even avoid it, it is happening every moment. We have made every arrangement to avoid it. We make our cemeteries outside the town, we make our graves with beautiful marble and we write beautiful maxims on that marble. We go and put flowers on graves. These are ways to make the shock of death a little less shocking. When a man dies we say that his soul is immortal. This is again a trick. I am not saying that the soul is not immortal – it is – but it is not for you, it is only for those who have awakened. You are simply using it as a consolation. It is a prop to avoid death.

We paint the dead man, we put beautiful clothes on the dead man. In the West now a whole profession exists of how to decorate the dead body so that it looks alive at least in appearance. And sometimes it happens that a dead body can be decorated so perfectly that the man never looked so radiant when he was alive as he looks when he is dead.

I have heard about a rich man. He purchased a beautiful Cadillac and just three days later he died. The doctors had said that the disease was so sudden that nothing could be done about it and he would die within twenty-four hours. So he made a will. He said, 'I have just purchased my Cadillac. It was specially ordered, made to order, and I have not even been able to drive it, so do one thing – bury me in my Cadillac.'

His will was followed. A big grave was dug and he was put in the Cadillac and with a crane the Cadillac was put in the grave. The whole town had gathered to see this thing. All were there.

Two beggars also came and one beggar said to the other, 'Man, that guy really knows how to live!'

It happens! You are so dead in life that sometimes your death can look very, very alive – comparatively.

You cannot solve the problem of death. There is no way. Then what is one supposed to do? The easiest way that man has found is to go into a sleep about death – not to look at it, to avoid it. Never look at it face to face, eye to eye. Avoid it. Avoidance has become the way of man.

There are problems – ill-health is there, disease is there,

cancer is there, tuberculosis is there, and many things. And nobody is ever secure, nobody can ever be – because life exists in insecurity. You may have a big bank balance but the bank can go bankrupt any day, or the country can become communist. Anything can happen. You have a wife and suddenly she falls in love with a stranger and is gone. Who knows? Life is insecure, there is no security. You can only pretend that you are secure, nothing ever is.

Then what to do? Escape into sleep. Create a haze around yourself so that you don't see clearly what is what. People live with this haze, this metaphysical haze, around themselves, like a fog, so they can believe whatsoever they want to believe.

I have heard about a man who was driving his car. A young hippie was standing on the road. He wanted to be taken into the car. The driver very lovingly opened the door and took him in. And the car started rushing again with mad speed.

It started raining. And as it started raining the driver speeded up. The wipers were not working. The hippie could not see at all through the windshield so he told the driver, 'The wipers are not working and you are going with such speed. I cannot see anything and my eyes are perfect and you are an old man, how are you managing?'

The driver laughed. He said, 'You don't be worried. It

does not matter whether the wipers are working or not because I have left my glasses at home.'

When you don't see, you think nothing matters. You create a fog around yourself then you don't see ahead. Death is there, you don't see; insecurity is there, you don't see; your wife is going to leave tomorrow, you don't see; your husband is going to become a poet, you don't see. There is a fog. You remain asleep.

Sleep is avoidance. It is a trick of the mind to avoid real problems in life. It is a drug invented by man. But it doesn't help. The reality remains as it is, the danger remains as it is, the insecurity remains as it is. In fact, it becomes worse because you are unaware. You could have done something, but now you cannot because you cannot see and you have created a fog. The problems are multiplied by your fog and your sleep, they are not solved. Nothing is solved by your sleep. But you can have a kind of consolation that there is no problem.

You must have heard about the ostrich and his logic. This is his logic: when the ostrich sees an enemy coming, he simply puts his head into the earth, into the sand. He stands there completely unafraid because he cannot see. His eyes are closed in the sand, he cannot see the enemy. And his logic is that if you cannot see, then the enemy is not.

This ostrich logic is very human. Don't laugh at the ostrich. This is what you have done, this is what millions of people have done, this is what ninety-nine percent of humanity is doing. Don't see the enemy; just go on believing everything is okay. At least this moment nothing is wrong, everything is okay, so why bother? Go on living in this drugged state.

But this is the sure way never to be in a mood of celebration. Never will you be able to celebrate because celebration comes through transcendence – when problems are transcended. Remember, I use the word 'transcendence' not the word 'solution'. No problem is ever solved, no problem can ever be solved – because to call them problems is, in fact, not right. They are not problems.

Try to understand it. Is insecurity a problem? We call it a problem but it is just the way life is. You don't say that the tree is green so green is a problem. It is just the way trees are. You don't say that the sun is hot so this is a problem. It is not a problem. The sun is hot – it is simply how the sun is. Insecurity is a basic ingredient of life. In fact, life cannot exist without insecurity. Without insecurity life will be dead – it is only through insecurity that it remains alive, throbbing, hopeful.

Insecurity makes it possible for life to change. Change is very essential. If you change, there will be insecurity; if you don't change, there is no insecurity – but if you don't change then you are a rock. A rock is more secure than a rose bush. Naturally, because a rock does not change so fast. For millions of years it can remain the same, there is no problem. But for the rose bush there are many problems. If water is not given to it for two days the roses will start disappearing, the greenery will start disappearing, the bush will start dying. Or, if the sun is too hot, or a madman comes, or an animal enters into the garden, then too it will die. The rose bush has to exist on so many insecurities – for the rock there is no problem. But the rose bush changes, that's why it is alive.

Animals are less alive, man is more alive – or at least can be. It is his potentiality to be more alive. But then there is more insecurity. No animal is aware of death, hence there is no problem. Only man is aware of death. But if you are aware of death then it can become a challenge – how to transcend it, how to face it, how to live in the face of death, not avoiding it, accepting it totally, knowing totally that it is there.

How to live knowing that death is going to happen? In fact, life will become a great intensity when death is known. You know that tomorrow it is possible that death may come – or maybe the next moment – so you have only one moment at one time in your hand. Don't waste it. And don't live lukewarmly because who knows? – the next moment may never come. This is the only moment that you have got, the next is not certain. It may be, it may not be, you cannot depend on it. You cannot postpone, you cannot sacrifice the present for the uncertain future. If you accept death and if you face death you will start living in the present. Death is not a problem, death will help you to be alive, more alive, intensely alive. You will start living totally because there is no way to have any hope for the future. The future does not exist. If death is known, accepted, then the future disappears.

And with the disappearance of the future the only thing that remains in your hands is now. Then you can go deep into this now – whatsoever you are doing. You can be eating or dancing or making love to a woman or singing or digging a hole in the ground – whatsoever you are doing. This is the only time you have, why not do it totally? Why not celebrate it? Celebration and being total mean the same thing. You celebrate only when you are total in something and when you are total in something you celebrate it.

Have you not watched it yourself? Whenever you are total in something there is celebration. For example, if listening to me you become a listener totally, there is great celebration. You are not doing anything, you are simply sitting there. But listening to me, deeply, totally, intensely, a great joy arises. And you are not doing anything, you are not creating that joy, the joy is already there – you just have to be here, here now. Here is the only space and now is the only time – because death is there.

To think of death as a problem is to move in the wrong direction. Then you start avoiding it. When you avoid it you become asleep. To accept death... Yes, death is there, it is part of life. It entered you the very day you were born, it entered with birth. Birth and death are two aspects of the same coin. The day you were born you became vulnerable to death. Now there is no way to avoid it.

Yes, I know medical science can help man to live for 200 or 300 years, but that doesn't make any difference. Whether you live for 30 years or 300 years does not make any difference. The difference can be made only by one thing – how you live, not how long. If you live sleepily you can sleep for 30 years or 300 years or 3,000 years, it doesn't matter. There will be no celebration. If you live a life totally, meditatively, then even three minutes may be enough, even a single second may be enough. A single second of total ecstasy gives you a taste of eternity. It is enough, more than enough. You will not hanker for anything more. It is so fulfilling, it is such a contentment.

Don't avoid, otherwise you will remain asleep. Don't avoid death, don't avoid problems, don't avoid anxieties – accept them, encounter them, they are part of the game.

The earth is like a ship on which one day you suddenly find yourself, not knowing from where you come, not knowing where you are going, seeing people becoming old, afflicted, seeing people die. You start inquiring and nobody is interested in your question. In fact, whenever you ask somebody 'What is death?' he starts feeling restless. He wants to avoid it, he wants to drop the topic. He will think you are a little morbid or something. Why bring up such an ugly subject? Why talk about death?

The very word *death* gives you a shiver in the spine. People don't use the word death when somebody has died, they say he has 'passed away.' Just to avoid the word death they say 'he has passed away,' or 'he has been called by God' or 'he has gone to his heavenly abode.' Tricky people. Just to avoid one single word *death*, to avoid the fact that he has died – because death can hurt you, that you have to die can hurt you – they say, 'He has gone to a heavenly abode. Now it is perfectly okay, let him go. He must be enjoying the company of God.' This is the situation.

And people are deeply involved in their games. Somebody is playing the game of politics – he wants to become the prime minister or the president or somebody. He is completely absorbed in it. Somebody is absorbed in his money game – how to have more money, how to grab more money. And somebody is absorbed in holding knowledge. These are all games and these games are invented by man to avoid real problems in life. These games give you a chance to solve things. You cannot solve anything in real life, nothing can be solved – because real life is a mystery not a problem. Death is a mystery not a problem. You cannot solve it. It is not a crossword puzzle. It is a mystery. It remains mysterious. You have to accept it as it is. There is no way to solve it. But through accepting it you transcend. Through accepting it a great transformation comes to you.

The problem remains there but it is no longer a problem. You are no longer against it. The very word *problem* shows that you are against it, afraid of it, it is the enemy. When you accept it, it becomes the friend, you befriend it. Insecurity is there but it is no more a problem. In fact, it gives you a thrill.

In fact, if your wife leaves you tomorrow, don't be worried about it. Let it be a thrill, let it be an adventure. Nothing is wrong in it. If your son turns out to be a hippie, don't be worried. At least he has done something that you never did. You missed something he is not going to miss.

Let him live in his own way. He has more life. He is more interested in real life than in your bogus games. You wanted him to become rich and he has become a beggar. You wanted him to become a president or a governor or some other nonsense and he has become a sannyasin: Don't be worried. It is not a problem at all. You have given birth to an alive person – be happy, feel thankful. It is good.

Maybe by his turning into these unknown paths some window will open in your mind also, some ray of light will enter into your dead being, you will start pulsating again. Who knows? You are not really dead, you have only become dead. You have gathered an armor around you which has become heavier and heavier every day and it is difficult to move with it. Seeing your son turn on to the unknown, maybe you will drop your armor, you will start moving for the first time into the labyrinth of the mysterious life. For the first time you become alert that the games you are playing are meaningless, they are just games.

Have you not watched people playing chess and how absorbed they become? And all is false. The king and the queen and the elephants and the horses... everything is false, just symbolic. But people get so absorbed in the symbols that they forget that life is real, not symbolic.

I have heard....

A motorist was driving along a country road when he saw a big sign: *Beware of the Dog*. Farther down the road was another sign in even bigger letters: *Beware of the Dog*. Finally he arrived at the farmhouse and there was a little poodle standing in front of the house.

'Do you mean to say,' asked the motorist, 'that that little dog keeps strangers away?'

'No,' replied the farmer, 'but the signs do.'

Who bothers to look at the dog? People have become so afflicted with signs, symbols, words, language – who bothers whether there is really a dog or not?

It works, I know, because I have practiced it. Once I used to live in a town and I didn't have a dog. But I used to put up a sign. There was no poodle, just a sign, a big sign, on the door: *Beware of the Dog*. And people wouldn't enter. That was enough to keep them away. You need not have a dog really. Who bothers about reality?

So people have gone into sleep because they are trying to avoid. And they are trying to avoid because they have wrongly taken mysteries as problems. Insecurity is mystery. Death is mystery. Love is mystery. All is mysterious. And by 'mysterious' I mean it is not logical. It is very illogical. One never knows.

Do you know when you fall in love with a woman or a man? Have you any answer why? Can you answer it? It simply happens. It simply happens out of the blue. You come across a strange woman and suddenly something has clicked. You can't answer, she can't answer. Suddenly you find yourself moving in a direction together. Suddenly you find you are on the same wavelength, you fit. And as suddenly it happens that it can disappear also. It is a mystery. You may live with a woman for 20 years, in deep love and with all the joys of love, and then one day that climate is no more there, that vibe is no more there. You are there, the woman is there, and it is not that you have not loved each other – you have loved for 20 years – but suddenly, as it came out of nothing, it disappears into nothing. It is not there. Now you can pretend – that's what husbands and wives go on doing. You can pretend. You can pretend that still the love is there but now life will become a drag. The joy is no more there.

Love cannot be pretended and love cannot be managed.

There is no way to manage love; it is bigger than you. It comes from the same source as birth and death. From where they come, love comes. These three things – birth, love and death – come from the unknown. They suddenly enter you like a breeze and they suddenly disappear.

You cannot solve these problems but you can transcend

them. And the way to transcend is to accept that they are there. And don't think that they are problems, they are mysteries. Once you start feeling that they are mysteries suddenly you are *en rapport* with life – and there is celebration, there is trust.

This is possible only if mind is not allowed to play games. The heart is the center where love happens, birth happens, death happens. When death happens it is the heart that stops. When love happens it is the heart that dances. When birth happens it is the heart that starts beating. All that is real happens in the heart and all that is unreal happens in the mind. The mind is the faculty for the unreal, for the fictitious, for the games.

Part Three

Proposals for a Golden Future

Up to now people have always been talking about the golden past. We have to learn the language of the golden future.

There is no need for you to change the whole world; just change yourself and you have started changing the whole world, because you are part of the world. If even a single human being changes, his change will radiate to thousands and thousands of others. He will become a triggering point for a revolution which can give birth to a new kind of human being.

Richness in All
Dimensions

Religion is the ultimate in luxury. The poor man has to think about bread and butter – he cannot even manage that. He has to think about a shelter, clothes, children, medicine, and he cannot manage these small things. His whole life is burdened by trivia; he has no space, no time to devote to God. And even if he goes to the temple or to the church, he goes to ask only for material things. His prayer is not true prayer, it is not that of gratitude; it is a demand, a desire. He wants this, he wants that – and we cannot condemn him, he has to be forgiven. The needs are there and he is constantly under a weight. How can he find a few hours just to sit silently, doing nothing? The mind goes on thinking. He has to think about the tomorrow.

Jesus says: Look at the lilies in the field; they toil not, they don't think of the morrow. And they are far more beautiful than even Solomon, the great king, in all his grandeur, ever was.

True, the lilies toil not and they don't think of the morrow. But can you say it to a poor man? If he does not think of the morrow, then tomorrow is death. He has to prepare for it; he has to think from where he is going to get his food. Where he is going to be employed – he has to think. He has children and a wife, he has an old mother and an old father. He cannot be like the lilies of the field. How can he avoid toil, labor, work? – that will be suicidal.

The lilies are certainly beautiful and I totally agree with Jesus, but Jesus' statement is not yet applicable to the greater part of humanity. Unless humanity becomes very rich, the statement will remain just theoretical; it will not have any practical use.

I would like the world to be richer than it is. I don't believe in poverty and I don't believe that poverty has anything to do with spirituality. Down the ages it has been told that poverty is something spiritual; it was just a consolation.

Just the other day, a French couple wrote a letter to me. They must be new arrivals here, they don't understand me. They must have come with certain prejudices. They were worried, very much worried. They wrote in the letter that, 'We don't understand a few things. Why does this place look so luxurious? This is against spirituality. Why do you drive in a beautiful car? This is against spirituality.'

Now, for these three or four days I have been driving in an Impala. It is not a very beautiful car; in America it is the car of the plumbers! But in a sense I am also a plumber – the plumber of the mind. I fix nuts and bolts. It is a poor man's car. In America, the people who use Chevrolet Impalas, etcetera, their neighborhood is called the 'Chevrolet neighborhood' – that means poor people's neighborhood.

But this French couple must have the old idea that poverty has something spiritual about it. Man has lived so long in poverty that he had to console himself, otherwise it would have been intolerable. He had to convince himself that poverty is spiritual.

Poverty is not spiritual – poverty is the source of all crimes. And I would like to tell the couple that if you want to cling to your beliefs and prejudices, this is not the place for you. Please get lost! – the sooner the better, because you may be corrupted here. Listening to me is dangerous for you.

To me, spirituality has a totally different dimension. It is the ultimate luxury – when you have all and suddenly you see that, although you have all, deep inside there is a vacuum which has to be filled, an emptiness which has to be transformed into a plenitude. One becomes aware of the inner emptiness only when one has everything on the outside. Science can do that miracle. I love science, because it can create the possibility for religion to happen.

Up to now, religion has not happened on the earth. We have talked about religion but it has not happened; it has not touched the hearts of the millions. Only once in a while a person has been able to become enlightened. In a big garden where millions of bushes and trees are, if only once in a while in thousands of years a flower comes to a tree, you will not call it a garden. You will not be thankful to the gardener. You will not say, 'The gardener is great, because look: after 1,000 years, out of millions of trees, one tree has again blossomed with one flower.' If this happens that simply shows it must have happened in spite of the gardener! Somehow he has forgotten about the tree, somehow he has neglected the tree, somehow the tree has escaped his grip.

Man has lived irreligiously: talking about God, certainly – going to the church, to the temple, to the mosque – yet his life showing no flavor of religiousness.

My vision of religion is totally different. It has nothing to do with poverty. I would like the whole earth to become as rich as paradise – richer than paradise – so that people can stop thinking about paradise. Paradise was created by poor people just to console themselves that, 'Here we are suffering, but it is not for long. Only a few days more, or a few years, and death will come and we will be transported into paradise.'

And what a consolation! – that those who are rich here will be thrown into hell. Jesus says a camel can pass through the eye of the needle, but the rich man cannot pass through the gate of heaven. What consolation! The poor people must have felt very satisfied, contented, that, 'It is only a question of a few days more: then you will be in hellfire and I will sit in the lap of God, with all the

luxuries, with all the riches, with all the joys that I am
deprived of here and you are enjoying.' The idea of
paradise seems to be just a revenge.

I would like *this earth* to be a paradise – and it cannot
happen without science. So how can I be anti-science? I
am not anti-science. But science is not all. Science can
create only the circumference; the center has to be that of
religiousness. Science is exterior, religion is interior. And I
would like men to be rich on both sides: the exterior
should be rich and the interior should be rich. Science
cannot make you rich in your inner world; that can be
done only by religion.

If science goes on saying there is no inner world, then I
am certainly against such statements – but that is not being
against science, just against these particular statements.
These statements are stupid, because the people who are
making these statements have not known anything of the
inner.

Karl Marx says religion is the opium of the people – and
he has never experienced any meditation. His whole life
was wasted in the British Museum, thinking, reading,
collecting notes, preparing for his great work, *Das Kapital*.
And he was so much into trying to gain more and more
knowledge that it happened many times – he would faint
in the British Museum! He would have to be carried

unconscious to his home. And it was almost an everyday thing that he would have to be forced to leave the museum – because the museum has to close sometime, it cannot remain open for twenty-four hours.

He had never heard about meditation; he knew only thinking and thinking. But still, in a way he is right, that the old religiousness has served as a kind of opium. It has helped poor people to remain poor; it has helped them to remain contented as they are, hoping for the best in the next life. In that way he is right. But he is not right if we take into consideration a Buddha, a Zarathustra, a Lao Tzu – then he is not right. And these are the really religious people, not the masses; the masses know nothing of religion.

I would like you to be enriched by Newton, Edison, Eddington, Rutherford, Einstein; and I would like you also to be enriched by Buddha, Krishna, Christ, Mohammed, so that you can become rich in both the dimensions – the outer and the inner. Science is good as far as it goes, but it does not go far enough – and it cannot go. I am not saying that it can go and it does not go – no. It *cannot* go into the interiority of your being. The very methodology of science prevents it from going in. It can go only outwards, it can study only objectively; it cannot go into the subjectivity itself. That is the function of the religious search.

The society needs science, the society needs religiousness. And if you ask me what should be the first priority – science should be the first priority. First the outer, the circumference, then the inner – because the inner is more subtle, more delicate.

Science can create the space for real religiousness to exist on the earth.

I am not in favor of those people who in the past, in the name of religion, became fixated in their introversion; that is another extreme. A few people are fixated as extroverts – as a reaction, a few other people become fixated as introverts. Both become dead. Life belongs to the flexible one who can move from extroversion to introversion and from introversion to extroversion as easily as you move outside your house and inside your house. When it is too cold inside you come out in the sun; when it becomes too hot you come inside under the shelter, in the coolness of the house – and there is no problem. It is as simple as that.

Meditation does not mean going against the outside world. It has been so in the past. That's why religion has failed, it could not succeed; it could not have succeeded in any way. Life belongs to the fluid, to the flowing.

Whenever you become fixated you become a thing.

Your monks were introverts; they closed their eyes to the outside world. That's why in the East we could not develop science, although the first steps were taken in the East. Mathematics was developed in India. The first steps towards technology were taken in China. But there it stopped for the simple reason that the greatest people in the East became fixated introverts; they lost interest in the objective world, they closed themselves totally to the objective. This is being only half of your total potential.

Now the West is doing just the opposite: it has become utterly extrovert, it does not know how to go in. It does not believe that there is any 'in,' it does not believe in any soul. It believes in man's behavior, not in man's inner existence. It studies the behavior and it says there is nobody inside it – it is all mechanical. Man has become a robot. If you don't know the soul, man becomes a robot. He is understood to be just a beautiful mechanism developed over millions of years – the long, long journey of evolution – but he is only a sophisticated machine.

Adolf Hitler could kill so many people so easily for the simple reason that if man is a machine, what is the harm in killing people? If you destroy your wristwatch you don't feel guilty; howsoever sophisticated it was, it was only a wristwatch. If you decided to destroy it, it is for you to decide; nobody can object to it. You cannot be dragged into a court as a murderer. Stalin could kill millions of people easily without any prick in his conscience for the simple reason that Marxism believes that there is no soul. Man is nothing but matter; consciousness is only a by-product of matter. This is one extreme.

Science has developed in the West, but religion has disappeared. In the East, religion developed but science disappeared. In both the ways man remains poor and half.

My effort is to create the whole man who will be able to be scientific and religious together.

A big, mangy dog was threatening a mother cat and her kittens. He had backed them into the corner of a barn, when suddenly the cat reared back on her hind legs and started barking and growling loudly. Startled and confused, the dog turned and ran from the barn, its tail tucked between its legs.

Turning to her kittens, the mother cat lifted a paw and told them, 'Now do you see the advantage of being bilingual?'

I want man to be bilingual. He should know science as much, as deeply, as he should know meditation. He should know mind as much as he should know meditation. He should know the language of the objective world – that is science – and he should know also the language of the subjective world – that is religion.

Only a man who is able to bridge the objective and the subjective, a man who is able to bridge the East and the West, a man who is able to bridge the materialist and the spiritualist, can be a whole man. The world is waiting for the whole man. If the whole man does not arrive soon, then there is no future for humanity. And the whole man can come only through deep, profound intelligence.

The earth is our home and we have to be earthly. A real spirituality must be rooted in earthliness. Any spirituality that denies the earth, rejects the earth, becomes abstract, becomes airy-fairy. It has no blood in it; it is no longer alive.

And what is wrong in having money? One should not be possessive; one should be able to use it. One should not be miserly. Money has to be created and money has to be used. Money is a beautiful invention, a great blessing, if rightly used. It makes many things possible. Money is a magical phenomenon.

If you have a hundred-dollar bill in your pocket, you have thousands of things in your pocket. You can have anything with those hundred dollars. You can materialize a man who will massage your body, or you can materialize food, or you can materialize *anything!* That hundred-dollar note carries many possibilities. You cannot carry all those possibilities with you if there is no note; then your life will be very limited. You can have a man who can massage your body, but then that is the only possibility you have. If you suddenly feel hungry or thirsty, then that man cannot do anything else. But a hundred-dollar note can do many things, millions of things; it has infinite possibilities. It is one of the greatest inventions of man; there is no need to be against it. I am not against it.

Use it. Don't cling to it. Clinging is bad. The more you cling to money, the poorer the world becomes because of your clinging, because money is multiplied if it is always moving from one hand to another hand.

In English we have another name for money which is more significant – it is 'currency.' That simply indicates that money should always remain moving like a current. It should always be on the move from one hand to another hand. The more it moves the better.

For example, if I have a hundred-dollar note and I keep it to myself, then there is only one hundred-dollar note in the world. If I give it to you and you give it to somebody else and each person goes on giving, if it goes through ten hands then we have a thousand dollars, we have used a thousand dollars' worth of utilities; the hundred dollars is multiplied by ten.

If you know how to use money; nothing is wrong in it. Yes, greed is bad. Greed means you become obsessed with money; you don't use it as a means, it becomes the end.

I am not against richness, I am in favor of religiousness. If you are very intelligent, then even in your poverty you can see the futility of riches. But then you have to be very perceptive: you have to think about something that you don't have, and you have to recognize that it is meaningless. Without having it, to recognize it as meaningless is very difficult. Having it and recognizing that it is meaningless is simple.

So I would like to repeat it again: if a poor person becomes religious that person shows intelligence, and if a rich person remains irreligious he shows stupidity. A rich man who is not religious simply means he is a fool. A poor man who is not religious simply needs sympathy; he is not a fool. You can forgive him. No rich person can be forgiven if he is not religious; that shows he is stupid: he has riches, and yet he has not been able to see that they are futile.

Your greed simply shows that you are feeling empty.

Now, you can fill it with things but it will never be filled. Or, you can start growing into your inward consciousness, and it will be filled.

People can continue for their whole lives wasting all their energies in greed, this ambition is not going to help you.

Science in
Service of Life

I would like all the scientists to listen to the heart. That will change the very character of science. It won't be in the service of death, it won't create more and more destructive weapons. It will be in the service of life. It will create better roses, more fragrant roses; it will create better plants, better animals, better birds, better human beings.

But the ultimate goal is to the center of one's being. And if a scientist is capable of using his head as far as the objective world is concerned, using his heart as far as the interpersonal world is concerned, and using his being as far as existence itself is concerned, then he is a perfect man.

My vision of the new man is of a perfect man: perfect in the sense that all his three dimensions – the head, the heart, and the being – are functioning without contradicting each other, but on the contrary, complementing each other.

The perfect man will create a perfect world. The perfect man will create a world of scientists, a world of poets, a world of meditators.

My approach is that all these three centers should be functioning in every person, because even a single individual is a world unto himself. And these centers are in the individual, not in the society; hence, my focus is on the individual. If I can change the individual, sooner or later the world is to follow. It will have to follow, because it will see the beauty of the new man.

The new man is not only clever in arithmetic, he can also enjoy and compose music. He can dance, he can play the guitar – which is a tremendous relaxation for his head, because the head is no longer functioning.

And the new man is not only of the heart; there are moments when he drops even deeper and simply is.

That source of your is-ness is the very center of your life. To touch it, to be there is to be rejuvenated. All the energies of your heart, of your head, will be tremendously multiplied, because you will be getting newer energy every day, every moment.

Right now, even a great scientist like Albert Einstein uses only fifteen percent of his potential. What to say about ordinary people? They never go beyond five to seven percent.

If all the three centers are functioning together, man will be able to function totally, one hundred percent. We can really create a paradise here, on this earth.

It is within our hands. Just a little effort, a little courage, and nothing more is needed.

The world has to be scientific for all the technologies, for all the comforts. The world has to be poetic; otherwise man becomes just a robot. The head is a computer. Without poetry and music and dance and song, what your head does can be done by a computer far more efficiently and infallibly. Popes have been declaring they are infallible. They are not. But if they want to be infallible, their brains can be replaced by a computer; then they will be infallible.

The heart is a totally different dimension of experiencing beauty, love, and expressing it. But that is not all. Unless you reach to your very center, you will remain discontented. And a discontented man is dangerous, because he will do anything to get rid of his discontentment.

The person who knows himself and his center is the richest. In fact, that's where the Kingdom of God is. It is your kingdom; there, you are a god. Deep down, centered in your being, you become an emperor.

Therefore, I say to the whole world that my empire consists only of emperors. And we have to expand the empire as quickly and as fast as possible, because the forces of death are coming closer every moment. But I have every hope and certainty that life cannot be defeated by death.

Life-affirmative people are needed. And if you are overflowing with life, it is contagious, it starts infecting other people.

So wherever you are, rejoice, celebrate. Help your love, your life, your laughter to spread all over the world.

It is possible. It has to be made possible.

We can do it! And there is nobody else to take the

responsibility. We are the only alternative. We are the answer to the questions that are surrounding humanity.

Science as it exists now is lopsided; it takes account only of the material, it leaves the spiritual out of it – and that is very dangerous.

If man is only matter, all meaning disappears from life. What meaning can life have if man is only matter? What poetry is possible, what significance, what glory? The idea that man is matter reduces man to a very undignified state. The so-called science takes all the glory of man away from him. That's why there is such a feeling of meaninglessness all over the world.

People are feeling utterly empty. Yes, they have better machines, better technology, better houses, better food, than ever. But all this affluence, all this material progress, is of no value unless you have insight – something that transcends matter, body, mind – unless you have a taste of the beyond. And the beyond is denied by science.

Science divides life into two categories: the known and the unknown. Religiousness divides life into three categories: the known, the unknown and the unknowable. Meaning comes from the unknowable. The known is that which was unknown yesterday, the unknown is that which will become known tomorrow. There is no qualitative difference between the known and the unknown, only a question of time.

The unknowable is qualitatively different from the known / unknown world. Unknowable means the mystery remains; howsoever deep you go into it, you cannot demystify it. In fact, on the contrary, the deeper you go, the more the mystery deepens. A moment comes in the religious explorer's life when he disappears into the mystery like a dewdrop evaporating in the morning sun. Then only mystery remains. That is the highest peak of fulfillment, of contentment; one has arrived home. You can call it God, nirvana, or whatsoever you like.

I am not against science – my approach is basically scientific. But science has limitations, and I don't stop where science stops; I go on, I go beyond.

Use science, but don't be used by it. It is good to have great technology; certainly it helps man to get rid of stupid work, certainly it helps man to get rid of many kinds of slavery. Technology can help man and animals both. Animals are also tortured; they are suffering very much because we are using them. Machines can replace them, machines can do all the work. Man and animals can both be free.

And I would like a humanity which is totally free from work, because in that state you will start growing – in aesthetic sense, sensitivity, relaxation, meditation. You will become more artistic and you will become more spiritual because you will have time and energy available.

I am not against science, I am not anti-science at all. I would like the world to have more and more of science, so that man can become available for something higher.

The new humanity will not have any jails and will not have any judges and will not have any legal experts. These are absolutely unnecessary, cancerous growths on the body of society. There will certainly have to be sympathetic scientists; meditative, compassionate beings, to work out why it happened that a certain man committed rape: is he really responsible? According to me, on no account is he responsible. Either he has committed rape because of the priests and the religions teaching celibacy, repression for thousands of years – this is the outcome of a repressive morality – or biologically he has hormones that compel him to commit rape.

Although you are living in a modern society, most of you are not contemporaries because you are not aware of the reality that science goes on discovering. Your educational system prevents you from knowing it, your religions prevent you from knowing it, your governments prevent you from knowing it.

To punish him is simply an exercise in stupidity. By punishing, you cannot change his hormones. Throwing him in jail, you will create a homosexual, some kind of pervert. In American jails they have done a survey: thirty percent of the inmates are homosexuals. That is according to their confession; we don't know how many have not confessed. Thirty percent is not a small number. In monasteries the number is bigger – fifty percent, sixty percent. But the responsibility lies with our idiotic clinging to religions, which are out of date, which are not supported and nourished by scientific research.

The new commune of man will be based on science, not on superstition. If somebody does something that is harmful to the community as such, then his body has to be looked into; he needs some physiological change or biological change. His mind has to be looked into – perhaps he needs some psychoanalysis. The deepest possibility is that neither the body nor the mind are of much help; that means he needs a deep spiritual regeneration, a deep meditative cleansing.

Instead of courts, we should have meditative centers of

different kinds, so every unique individual can find his own way. And we will have – instead of law experts, who are simply irrelevant; they are parasites sucking our blood – scientific people of different persuasions in the courts, because somebody may have a chemical defect, somebody may have a biological defect, somebody may have a psychological defect. We need all these kinds of experts, of all persuasions and schools of psychology, all types of meditators, and we can transform the poor people who have been victims of unknown forces... and have been punished by us. They have suffered in a double sense.

First, they are suffering from an unknown biological force. Secondly, they are suffering at the hands of your judges, who are nothing but butchers, henchmen; your advocates, all kinds of your law experts, your jailers – it is simply so insane that future human beings will not be able to believe it. It is almost the same with the past.

Just the other day there was a report from South India that a woman was thought to be having intercourse with the devil. Now the devil has been almost dead for many centuries; suddenly he became alive in that small village? And the villagers took the woman to the priest who declared that she should be hung upside down from a tree and beaten: the devil is still inside her. Somebody informed the police of the nearby town. The police arrived, but the villagers were reluctant.... Two hundred villagers were standing, stopping the police, saying, 'You cannot interfere with our religious conceptions.' And they were beating the woman – they killed her! Until she was dead, they were not satisfied. They could not find the devil, but they killed the woman.

This used to be the common practice all over the world. Mad people were beaten to cure their madness; people who were schizophrenic, who were thought to be possessed by ghosts, were beaten almost to death – this was thought to be the treatment. Millions of people have died because of your great treatments.

Now we can simply say that those people were barbarous, ignorant, primitive. The same will be said about us. I am already saying it: that your courts are barbarous, your laws are barbarous. The very idea of punishment is unscientific. There is nobody in the world who is a criminal; everybody is sick, and needs sympathy and a scientific cure, and half of your crimes will disappear.

Private property creates thieves, robbers. Once private property disappears.... And in a commune there is going to be no private property, everything belongs to all; naturally, stealing will disappear. You don't steal water and accumulate it, you don't steal air. A commune has to create everything in such abundance that even the stupid person cannot think of accumulating it. What is the point? It is always available, fresh. Money has to disappear from society. A commune does not need money. Your needs should be fulfilled by the commune. All have to produce, and all have to make the commune richer, affluent, accepting the fact that a few people will be lazy. But there is no harm in it.

In every family, you will find somebody lazy. Somebody is a poet, somebody is a painter, somebody simply goes on playing on his flute – but you love the person. A certain percentage of lazy people will be respectfully allowed. In fact, a commune that does not have lazy people will be a little less rich than other communes which have a few lazy people who do nothing but meditate, who do nothing but go on playing on their guitar while others are toiling in the fields. A little more human outlook is needed; these people are not useless. They may not seem to be productive of commodities, but they are producing a certain joyful, cheerful atmosphere. Their contribution is meaningful and significant.

With the disappearance of money as a means of exchange, many crimes will disappear. And when from the very beginning every child is brought up with a reverence for life – reverence for the trees because they are alive, reverence for animals, reverence for birds – do you think such a child one day can be a murderer? It will be almost inconceivable.

And if life is joyous, full of songs and dances, do you think somebody will desire to commit suicide? Ninety percent of crimes will disappear automatically; only ten percent of crimes may remain, which are genetic, which need hospitalization – but not jails, prisons, not people to be sentenced to death. This is all so ugly, so inhuman, so insane.

The new man can live without any law, without any order. Love will be his law, understanding will be his order. Science will be, in every difficult situation, his last resort.

I can understand the concern about the misuse of genetic engineering; it is my concern too. But there are many things to be understood. The first is, never act out of fear. If man had acted out of fear there would have been no progress possible.

For example, the people who invented bicycles ... can you ever think of any danger? It is simply inconceivable that bicycles can be dangerous. But then the Wright brothers made the first flying machine out of the parts of bicycles. The whole world rejoiced – because nobody could have foreseen that airplanes would be used to destroy cities, millions of people, in the First World War.

But the same airplanes are carrying millions of people around the world. They have made the world small, they have made it possible to call the world just a global village. They have made bridges between peoples, they have brought together people of different races, religions, languages in such a way that no other invention has been able to do. So the first thing to remember is that acting out of fear is not the right way.

Act cautiously, with consciousness, remembering the possibilities and the dangers, and creating the atmosphere to prevent those dangers. Now, what can be more dangerous than nuclear weapons in the hands of the politicians? You have put the most dangerous thing into their hands.

Now, in fact there is no need to be afraid; even nuclear weapons can be used creatively. And I have a deep trust in life, that they will be used creatively. Life cannot allow itself to be destroyed so easily, it is going to give tremendous resistance. In that resistance is hidden the birth of a new man, of a new dawn, of a new order, of the whole of life and existence.

According to me, nuclear weapons have made a great war impossible. Gautam Buddha could not do it, Jesus

Christ could not do it. All the saints of the world together have been talking about nonviolence, no war; they could not succeed. But nuclear weapons have done their job.

Seeing that the danger is so great, all the politicians are trembling deep down, that if a third world war begins the whole of life will be destroyed – and they will be included in it. They cannot save themselves. Nothing can be saved. This is a great chance for all those who love creation. This is the moment when we can turn the whole trend of science towards creativity.

Remember one thing, that science is neutral. It simply gives you power. Now, how to use it depends on you, depends on the whole of humanity and its intelligence. Science gives us more power to create a better life, to create more comfortable living, to create more healthy human beings. So, rather than preventing, just out of fear that some totalitarian power may misuse it....

Everything can be misused. And everything that can harm can also be of tremendous benefit. Don't condemn anything, just raise the consciousness of human beings.

What is needed is not to go backwards; otherwise you will destroy the whole of humanity. What is needed is to go forwards and learn some lesson from the past: so that, as scientific technology develops, simultaneously human consciousness should develop. And that will be the protection against technology being used as something harmful to mankind.

So one should not act out of fear; one should see the whole perspective. If there is fear, it comes not from the power generated by science; the fear comes from the unconscious man. In his hands everything becomes poisonous, dangerous.

Change the man, don't stop progressive science.

The world can be such a beautiful place. But certainly there are risks and there are dangers, and I am aware of them more than you are aware of them. But still, I want to take all the risks because man has nothing to lose – he has got nothing now, so why be so much afraid? He has everything to gain and he has nothing to lose.

The risk can be taken – yes, with consciousness, with awareness. Hence I am teaching all the time how to be more aware, how to be more conscious, because much has to be done once we have a certain portion of humanity alert and conscious. Those will be our guardians, our guards against technology being used in any way for evil purposes.

We can take every protective measure, but we cannot go backwards.

Education
for Life

The child needs your love, not your help.

The child needs nourishment, support, but not your help.

The natural potential of the child is unknown, so there is no way to help him rightly to attain to his natural potential. You cannot help when the goal is unknown; all that you can do is not interfere. And in fact, in the name of help everybody is interfering with everybody else; and because the name is beautiful, nobody objects.

Up to seven years, if a child can be left innocent, uncorrupted by the ideas of others, then to distract him from his potential growth becomes impossible. The child's first seven years are the most vulnerable. And they are in the hands of parents, teachers, priests ....

How to save children from parents, priests, teachers is a question of such enormous proportion that it seems almost impossible to find how to do it.

It is not a question of helping the child, it is a question of protecting the child.

If you have a child, protect the child from yourself! Protect the child from others who can influence him: at least up to seven years, protect him. The child is just like a small plant, weak, soft: just a strong wind can destroy it, any animal can eat it up. You put a protective wiring around it, but that is not imprisoning, you are simply protecting.

When the plant is bigger, the wires will be removed.

Protect the child from every kind of influence so that he can remain himself – and it is only a question of seven years, because by seven years he will be well grounded, centered, strong enough. You don't know how strong a seven-year-old child can be because you have not seen uncorrupted children, you have seen only corrupted children. They carry the fears, the cowardliness, of their fathers, mothers, their families. They are not their own selves.

If a child remains uncorrupted for seven years .... You will be surprised to meet such a child. He will be as sharp as a sword. His eyes will be clear, his insight will be clear. And you will see a tremendous strength in him, which you cannot find even in a seventy-year-old adult because the foundations are shaky. So in fact as the building goes on becoming higher and higher, the more and more shaky it becomes.

So you will see, the older a person becomes, the more afraid. When he is young he may be an atheist; when he becomes old he starts believing in God. Why is that?

When he is below thirty he is a hippie. He has courage to go against the society, to behave in his own way: to have long hair, to have a beard, to roam around the world, to take all kinds of risks. But by the time he is forty, all that has disappeared. You will see him in some office in a gray suit, clean shaven, well groomed. You will not even be able to recognize that he is an ex-hippie.

Where have all the hippies disappeared to? Suddenly you see them with a great force; then, just like used bullet cases, empty cartridges, impotent, defeated, depressed – trying to make something out of life, feeling that all those years of hippiedom were a wastage. Others have gone far ahead; somebody has become the president, somebody has become the governor, and 'we were stupid; we were just playing the guitar and the whole world passed us by.' They repent. It is really difficult to find an old hippie.

If you are a parent you will need this much courage – not to interfere. Open doors of unknown directions to the child so he can explore. He does not know what he has in him, nobody knows. He has to grope in the dark. Don't make him afraid of darkness, don't make him afraid of failure, don't make him afraid of the unknown. Give him support. When he is going on an unknown journey, send him with all your support, with all your love, with all your blessings.

Don't let him be affected by your fears.

The ordinary human being stops his growth of intelligence at the age of 14 because the biological purpose is complete. At the age of 14, the person is mature enough to give birth, to reproduce. Biology is no longer interested beyond this point.

This is the reason why the average human being is stuck at the age of 14 as far as his mental age is concerned. People go on growing physically up to 70, 80, 90, 100 years – in some places like Caucasia, up to 150, even 180. But their mental age remains stuck at 14. This has been the routine up to now.

This can be changed. And this should be changed because there is infinite potential for growth, but the change will come only if you have some goals beyond biology. If your life remains concerned only with sex, children, family, food, house, then there is no need; that much intelligence is enough. But if your interest is that of an Albert Einstein then your intelligence starts moving sometimes even ahead of your physical body.

Emerson is reported to have said – and rightly so – when asked how old he was: 'Three hundred and sixty years.'

The journalist who was asking said, 'Three hundred and sixty? You don't look more than sixty.'

Emerson said, 'That's right. From one point of view, I am 60 years old. But I have done so much work as far as my intelligence is concerned that either six people would be needed to do it or I would need 360 years. My intelligence is so far ahead of my physical body.'

Intelligence depends what you are doing with it.

The person who is meditating has the greatest possibility of reaching the highest peaks of intelligence because in meditation he is doing the greatest possible work that a man is capable of – and that is realizing oneself, knowing 'Who am I.' Entering into the deepest interiority of one's subjectivity is the greatest work for intelligence. Then you cannot even count – you cannot count Gautam Buddha's intelligence, it is beyond calculations, beyond measurements.

And if you are a meditator, as your meditation goes on becoming more and more luminous, your intelligence will be growing to the last breath of your life. Not only that, even after the last breath your intelligence will continue to grow – because you are not going to die, only your body will be dying. And the body has nothing to do with intelligence, mind has nothing to do with intelligence.

Intelligence is the quality of your awareness – more aware, more intelligent.

And if you are totally aware, you are as intelligent as this whole existence is.

The whole system of education has to be changed from the very roots. In short... we prepare people in education for livelihood rather than life. For 25 years we prepare – that is one third of the life – for livelihood. We never prepare people for death, and life is only 70 years; death is the door to eternity. It needs tremendous training.

According to me – and I feel with great authority that this is going to happen in the future if man survives – that education should be cut into pieces: 15 years for livelihood, and again after 42 years, 10 years in preparing for death. Education should be divided in two parts. Everybody goes to the university – of course to different universities, or to the same university but to different departments. One is to prepare children for life and one is to prepare people who have lived life and now want to know something more, beyond life.

Then the generation gap will disappear. Then the people who are of an older age will be more quiet, more silent, more peaceful, more wise; their advice will be worth listening to. Just sitting at their feet will be a great blessing; the respect for the old will return. Except this, there is no other way.

Education divided in two parts means young people study for life, and middle-aged people study for death. Of course, the middle-aged people will be studying meditation, singing, dancing, laughing; they will be learning celebration. They have to make their death a festival – that should be the goal of the second part of education.

They will paint, they will play music, they will sculpt, they will compose poetry; they will do all kinds of creative things. Livelihood they have managed; now their children are doing that. Geography, history and all kinds of idiotic subjects, their children are learning. Let them know where Timbuktu is.

I have always wondered why – with my geography teacher I was continually in conflict – 'Why should I know where Timbuktu is? What business is it of mine?'

He said, 'You are strange, nobody has ever asked this.'

I said, 'I am going to ask on every point... Constantinople, which in Hindi becomes even worse: Kustuntunia. I have no business with these things. Teach me something valuable.'

And my geography teacher used to hit his head... he would say, 'The whole of geography is this!'

The history teacher was teaching about the ugliest people that have existed in the world. From the history teacher I never got any idea about Bodhidharma or Zarathustra or Baal Shemtov or Lin Chi or Chuang Tzu; I never got any idea, and these are the people who have made humanity evolve.

But I have heard about Tamerlane. Do you know what *lang* means? He was one-legged. It is Tamurlang. Giving him respect, nobody called him 'one-legged Tamer' but he created so much nuisance that very few people can be compared with him. And for almost three generations... his son was worse than him, and his grandson defeated both.

About these people, who were just murderers and criminals, the whole history is full. And they are called emperors, conquerors, 'Alexander the Great.' Even if they were really bad, still history repeats their names, their great acts: 'Ivan the Terrible!'

This kind of history is bound to create wrong kinds of people in the world. All these histories should be burned simultaneously all over the world, so all these names disappear completely. And they should be replaced by those beautiful people who have all the credit for your being human. They are the people who have made humanity worthy of respect, who have given it a dignity and a pride, and who have opened doors of mysteries, of the beyond.

The second part of education should consist of meditativeness, of awareness, of witnessing, of love, of compassion, of creativity – and certainly we will again be without any generation gap. The younger person will respect the older person, and not for any formal reasons but actually because the old person is respectable. He knows something beyond the mind and the young person knows only something within the mind.

The young person is still struggling in the trivia of the world, and the older person has gone beyond the clouds; he has almost reached to the stars. It is not a question of etiquette to respect him. You are bound to respect him, it is absolutely a compulsion of your own heart – not a formality taught by others.

In my childhood... in India it is an absolute formality: anybody who comes as a guest, you have to touch their feet. Before my father became completely aware of my behavior he used to push down my head: 'Touch the feet, the guest is God. And he is an old relative, you should follow the custom.'

One day a male goat with a beard entered just in my house. I touched his feet. My father said, 'What are you doing?'

I said, 'A guest is a God – and moreover with a beard! An old goat needs respect. You come here and touch his feet.'

He said, 'Your mind functions in a very different way than anybody else's.'

I said, 'You have to understand it: from now onwards if I meet an old dog on the road I'm going to touch his feet, an old donkey and I'm going to touch his feet. What is the difference between an old dog, an old donkey, and your old guest? To me they look all the same. In fact the old donkey looks so philosophical; the old dog looks so ferocious, like a warrior – they have some qualities. That old fellow that you were forcing my head down for.... Next time you force my head down you will repent!'

He said, 'What are you going to do?'

I said, 'I will show you, because I believe in doing things, not in saying things.'

Next time one of my faraway relatives came and my father forgot. He pushed my head down. And I had a big needle ready in my hand, so I pushed the needle into the old man's foot. He shrieked. He almost jumped. My father said, 'What has happened?'

I said, 'I have warned you, but you never listened. I don't have any respect for this person. I don't know him, I have never seen him before; why should I touch his feet? I am ready to touch the feet of someone whom I feel is respectable.' He understood that it is better not to force me because this was dangerous. Blood was coming out of that old man's foot.

I never stood in my university classes when the professors entered. In India you have to stand up. The professors looked immediately at me – forgot everybody else; they focused on me. And if it was just the beginning of the year they would ask, 'Why are you not standing?'

I said, 'There is no reason.'

And the professor would say, 'You don't understand. Have you never stood before in any class?'

I said, 'Never, because I don't find any reason. I'm perfectly at ease.'

He said, 'You.... How to make you understand that when a professor enters into the class, out of respect you have to stand up?'

I said, 'That's right. But I have not seen yet anything respectable in you. If I see something, I will stand up. And remember: there should not be double standards.'

'You mean...' he said, 'what do you mean?'

I said, 'I mean if I enter the class, you have to stand up – of course, only if you see something respectable in me. Otherwise there is no question, you can remain sitting down, or if you want you can even sleep. I don't care a bit.'

My professors used to try to persuade me. Once in a while the vice-chancellor would come on a round, and they would try to persuade me that 'Just for once... we don't want you to stand for us, but when the vice-chancellor comes into the class, don't create a fuss. Because then nothing else happens except the discussion about it.'

I said, 'I am helpless. I cannot do anything against my will. Let the man come. If I feel that he is respectable I will stand up. You don't have to tell me.'

And the first vice-chancellor under whom I was studying, the first time he came into the class he was drunk. And I am so allergic that I immediately felt that he was drunk. I remained sitting. The teacher looked at me, stared at me, gave indications that 'You stand up.' I remained sitting. When everybody was told to sit down, then I stood up.

I said, 'Now is the time for me to stand up. This man is drunk. It does not matter who he is, I am going to report him to the police.'

And the vice-chancellor was so much afraid and so nervous.... He had put his hat on the table. In a hurry he took my professor's hat and went out of the class. And my professor was running behind him to say, 'You are taking my hat.'

I said, 'You see what happens when you are drunk? That man has not even the guts to remain here and you wanted me to stand for him?'

The generation gap exists simply because the reason for respect has disappeared. Unless you create the reason again, the respect will not return. On the contrary, every kind of disrespect will take place. But it is possible to change the whole system.

I would love that the older people be not just old but also wise, not just in age but also in understanding, not only horizontally old but also vertically old... not only growing old but growing up also.

A society where old people are still behaving like young fools is not a society worth calling cultured or civilized. Old people should behave like enlightened people – not only behave, they should be enlightened. They should become a light to those who are still young and under biological infatuations, natural bondages. They have gone beyond; they can become guiding stars.

When education for death and education for livelihood are separated, when everybody goes twice to the university – first to learn how to go around this world of trivia and the second time to learn about eternity – the gap will disappear. And it will disappear in a beautiful way.

The End of Nations

You have to understand one thing: if the world is really interested in enjoying freedom, then politics should not be so important; it should be dethroned, reduced in power – there is no reason that it should have power. The government should be only functional, just as the post office is functional. Nobody knows who the postmaster general is. Give politicians good and great names, but there is no need to take them too seriously and waste all your newspaper front pages on these people who have been torturing humanity for centuries.

Start different ways of expression, creativity, that have nothing to do with politics. Start small guilds, small communes of painters, of poets, of sculptors, of dancers, who have nothing to do with politics, who have no desire to be powerful, who really want to live, and live fully.

Let the whole society be slowly divided into communes of creative people. There is no need for political parties in the world. Every individual should stand on his own merit. And people can choose. Why should there be a political party? There is no reason. If you need a finance minister, all the great experts you have in economics and finance can compete for it, and someone can be chosen for it. There is no need for any party. We should move from party politics to pure individuals – from democracy, from dictatorship, to meritocracy.

Merit should be the only decisive point. And we have so many people of great merit – but they should not become part of a political party, they should not degrade themselves. To become part of a political party is below them – to beg for votes and promise you false things, which they cannot fulfill. So only the third-class people, very mediocre people, become part of political parties; the best remain out.

The best should be the ones who manage the society. We have in every field geniuses, but you don't find those geniuses becoming prime ministers or presidents. They can become presidents and prime ministers if there are no political parties. Then their sheer merit will be enough, and nobody will even be capable of competing with them. They will not have to go to beg for your votes, they will be chosen unanimously.

There is no need to be a pessimist, no need to feel frustrated. After so long a history of continuous failure, I can understand, it is natural. But it is not going to help. We have to find a way... we have to find out why old attempts have failed, and we have to work out new methods, new strategies. The youth of the whole world are all in the same situation and are ready to change all old structures and make every change that helps humanity to become free.

Freedom is such a spiritual necessity that without it man never attains his humanity. Liberation from dead superstitions, ideologies, dogmas is such a great necessity that once you are free of it you will feel as if you have got wings and you can fly into the sky.

I love Bakunin and his philosophy of anarchism, but he is an impractical, unpragmatic philosopher. He simply goes on praising the beauties of anarchism: no government, no armies, no police, no courts. And I absolutely agree with him. But he had no idea and no plan for how this dream could be made into a reality.

Looking at man, you will need the government; looking at man, you will need the police. Otherwise there will be a multiplication of murders, rapes, thefts... life will be a chaos. Anarchism would not come, only a chaos. People would start making gangs, those gangs would exploit the weaker people and life would not become better, it would become worse.

Bakunin's anarchism is a utopia, a great dream. My own understanding is if we can transform man, if we can bring more and more people to meditation, if we can make more and more people unrepressed, living an authentic, natural life, sharing their love, having a great compassion for everything living, a reverence for life itself....

These individual revolutionaries, these individual rebels will be not just political rebels, they will be also rebelling against all the past conditionings. Mostly they will be religious rebels; they will be finding their own center of being. There are more and more people who are becoming individuals who can rejoice, and who are not going to betray the earth; who are not in favor of any unnatural way of life preached by all the religions. If these individuals spread around the world like a wildfire, then anarchism will be a by-product, not the goal.

For Bakunin it is the goal. He hates governments so much – and he is perfectly right in his hate, because governments have been doing so much harm to the individuality of people. He is against all laws, courts and judges, because these are not to protect justice, not to protect the weak, not to protect the victim – they are there to protect the power, the establishment, the rich. Behind the name of justice, they are enacting a tremendous conspiracy against man.

And Bakunin has no idea why men become rapists, he is not a psychologist. He is a great philosopher of anarchism. The future will owe tremendous respect to people like Bakunin, Bukharin, Tolstoy, Camus, because although they were not very scientific thinkers at least they created the idea. Without providing the foundation, they started talking about the temple.

My whole effort is not to bother about the temple but to make a great foundation; then, to raise the temple is not difficult. Anarchism will be a by-product of a society that is free from religions and religious superstitions; that is psychologically healthy, non-repressive; that is spiritually healthy, not schizophrenic; that knows the beauties of the outside world and also the inner treasures of consciousness, awareness. Unless these people exist first, anarchism is not possible; it can come only as a by-product.

The idea of rebellion is not new, but the idea of rebellion combined with enlightenment is absolutely new – it is my contribution. And if we can make the majority of humanity more conscious, more aware, with a few individuals reaching to the highest peak of enlightenment, then their rebellion will bring anarchism just like a shadow, following on its own accord.

It is good that the family is disappearing.

And with it nations will disappear, because the family is the unit of the nation.

So I am tremendously happy whenever I see the family disappearing, because I know behind it will go the nation. With it will go the so-called religions, because it is the family that imposes religion, nationality, and all kinds of things on you. Once the family is gone, who is going to force Christianity on you, Hinduism on you; who is going to insist that you are an American, that you are an Indian?

Once the family is gone, much of psychological disease will be gone, much of political insanity will be gone. You should be happy that they are disappearing.

Marriage was an invention against nature. It has tortured man long enough, but there was a time when it was needed. It was needed because there were powerful people and there were weaker people. The powerful people used to collect all the beautiful women for themselves, and the weaker people remained without wives. Their biology remained unsatisfied. So marriage had to be invented – it was invented by the weaker men. The weaker men got together, must have got together some time in the past and must have decided on it, because when weaker men are together then the stronger man is no longer the stronger. He is stronger than a single man, but he is not stronger than the whole mass of weak people.

The weak people got together and they said, 'One man, one wife' – because that is the ratio in which children are born. It was enforced by the weaker man over the stronger people; otherwise it was bound to be that they would collect all the beautiful women to their harem and the weaker people would remain sex-starved. That situation was not good. The family helped, and the monogamous family came into being. It was of great importance that the weaker people were no longer sex-starved.

But now the family is no longer needed, now it is phony. It is possible now that the woman can earn, the man can earn; they need not depend on each other. It is possible for a woman not to have children. It is possible for a woman to hire another woman to have her children grow in the other woman's womb, or she can arrange for a test-tube baby. Sex and children are no longer connected. You can have sex and it does not mean that you have to suffer children too. Now the family is absolutely out of date.

The commune has future. A commune means many independent individuals, not belonging to each other in the old ways of family, tribe, religion, nation, race – no. Only in one way are they related to each other: that is they are all independent. They respect your independence, and the same they expect from you: to respect their independence. That is the only relationship, the only friendship, the only thing that is the cementing force in a commune: that we respect each other's individuality, independence. The other's way of life, his style of life is absolutely accepted, respected.

The only condition is that nobody is allowed to interfere with anybody else in any sense.

So it is good that all this dead past is disappearing, and freeing us to create a new man, a new humanity, a new world.

The best government is no government.

The very idea of somebody governing somebody else is inhuman.

Government is a game, the ugliest and the dirtiest game in the world. But there are people in the lowest state of consciousness who enjoy it: these are the politicians. The only joy of a politician is to govern, to be in power, to enslave people

The greatest desire of all those who have reached to the peaks of consciousness has been the dream that one day we can get rid of all governments. That day will be the greatest in the whole history – past, present, future – of man, because getting rid of all governments will mean destroying the ugliest game, the game the politicians have been playing for centuries.

They have made man just a chess piece, and they have created so much fear, fear that without government there will be anarchy, disorder, chaos ... everything will be destroyed. And the strangest thing is that we go on believing this nonsense.

Just look at the past 5,000 years. Can you conceive that if there was no government at all in the world things would have been worse? In what way? In 3,000 years, 5,000 wars have been fought. Do you think more would have been possible without government – that more chaos was possible, more crime was possible?

What have these governments done? They have not done anything for the people except exploit them, exploit their fear, and set them against each other. A continuity of war somewhere or other on the earth is almost an absolute necessity for politicians to exist.

When I say no government is the best government I know perfectly well that perhaps it will not ever be possible. But it is better to have dreams that are impossible but are of some higher consciousness, of beauty, love. Perhaps if the idea goes on existing, some day we may come close to it. We may not be able to achieve it in its totality – hence I say, the closest to no government is one government, which is not impossible. And after one government, no government becomes very possible.

Try to understand the idea. When I say one government, then politics loses much juice. When there are so many presidents in the world and so many prime ministers and kings and queens, and everybody is trying to prove himself the greatest, the game has some juice. When there is one government then it becomes functional; there is nobody against it.

The whole joy of politics is in 'the enemy.' When there is no enemy, then you are just working like the Red Cross Society or the organization of post offices or railways or airplanes. Do you know who is the head of the organization that runs the railway trains? There is no need, he is just a functional head.

And when there is one government we can make it a Rotary Club. There is no need for anybody to remain a president for four or five years. A few weeks will be enough; enjoy four weeks and then rotate. There is no problem in it. So every part of the world is represented; sometimes their person is the president. But by the time the world comes to know, he is no longer the president. And when it is a Rotary Club people lose that desire, the will to power.

One government means that nations disappear.

In fact there is no validity for nations; they are simply a calamity.

People in poor countries like Ethiopia are dying of

starvation, and in Europe they are throwing foodstuff into the ocean. Because they have so much, that if they continue to keep it the prices in the market will go down – and prices have to be kept going up. The only way is to get rid of it. So much is being thrown away that just to throw it in the ocean 100,000 dollars are needed – just for the labor of throwing it into the ocean.

This is a mad world. Ethiopia is so close to Europe – for 100,000 dollars all that stuff could have reached Ethiopia. And it is not a small amount: millions of tons of food.

Can you believe human beings can be so inhuman when people are simply starving and dying just because there is no food in their country? People don't have water to drink – they are dying of thirst. And you are throwing food in the ocean!

This is what your nations have been doing.

The Power of
Consciousness

All our tangles in life are created by our unconsciousness, so the moment you become conscious those tangles disappear. It is not the power of consciousness that makes them disappear. It is the power of unconsciousness that creates them.

All the tangles of life, of love, of relationship are created by our unconsciousness. We don't know what we are doing, and by the time we become aware it is too late. What has been done cannot be undone. Our unconsciousness is very supportive to the ego – they have a co-existence. Coming of consciousness will not only disperse all the tangles, it will also disperse you as an ego. It is a very complicated and complex phenomenon.

In your unconsciousness you do something. It is almost certain that once you have done something wrong that has created misery in you, around you, you will come to your senses. But you cannot undo it because the ego comes in between. You cannot even say, 'I am sorry.' Just a simple apology may disperse the tangle but the ego won't allow even that. And you are almost a victim; you are not doing things. Your unconsciousness, your unawareness goes on forcing you to do things.

And when you bring light, naturally you see all the tangles of your life: how you yourself have created your misery, your suffering, your anguish. Seeing it is enough – all those tangles disappear.

A conscious man never creates any tangle. He lives more intensely than anybody else, but his life is without any tangles for the simple reason that in consciousness you cannot create tangles.

Two women are talking in a tearoom at four o'clock over two large, gooey ice cream sundaes and little sugary cakes. They have not seen each other since high school days and one is bragging about her very advantageous marriage.

'My husband buys me whole new sets of diamonds when the ones I have get dirty,' she says, 'and I have never even bothered to clean them.'

'Fantastic,' said the other woman.

'Yes,' says the first, 'we get a new car every two months.'

'Fantastic,' says the other.

'And our house...' pursues the first woman, 'Well, what is the use of talking about it, it is just...'

'Fantastic,' finishes the other.

'Yes, and tell me, what are you doing nowadays?' asked the first woman.

'I go to charm school,' says the other.

'Charm school! Why, how quaint. What do you learn there?'

'Well, we learn to say 'fantastic' instead of 'bullshit'.'

In your unconsciousness everything is bullshit. And when you become conscious, it is *really* fantastic: all tangles disappear, all problems disappear.

Gautam Buddha used to say that when the lights are on and from the windows people can see that the master is awake, thieves don't come close. When the lights are put off, only then do thieves come close to the house to see whether the master has gone to sleep and it is the right time to enter. He was saying this about consciousness. He used to call sex, greed, lust for power, position, respectability, all thieves. They come to you only when they see that there is no light in the man; inside it is all dark.

Once you are radiating consciousness and light, those thieves don't come close to you. Consciousness has its own power. And it is simply in the presence of consciousness that tangles disappear. The power is not used for dispersing the tangles and problems; the power is to bring blissfulness. The power is to bring peace, silence, at-homeness, at easeness and a tremendous ecstasy, a divine drunkenness.

Life becomes for the first time self-oriented; you don't have to beg from others for anything. Nobody can give you blissfulness; nobody can give you ecstasy. Nobody can give you the sense of immortality and the dance that comes with it. Nobody can give you the silence, which becomes a song in your heart.

What can people give to you? In fact, the power of consciousness gives you so much that you become capable of sharing with people. For the first time, you can give to people. They are living in darkness; they haven't seen any light. They don't have any idea what a conscious being is. They don't have any conception, comprehension of the power of consciousness, how many flowers shower, how much fragrance becomes natural to you.

You can give, and you can give them a taste and you can give them a direction, so they can also find the same power, which is dormant in them.

A conscious man, awakened, can help millions of people to move towards the source of joy, real and authentic life, to pure love, which knows nothing of hate, which knows nothing of jealousy, which has nothing to do with body and biology – which is just a spiritual communion, a feeling of deep compassion for your innermost being.

Yes, the power of consciousness gives you many things. The treasure is inexhaustible. But your problems and tangles that have been created by unconsciousness – for them no power is needed, just the presence of consciousness is enough.

Everyone is born enlightened. Everyone is born absolutely innocent, absolutely pure, absolutely empty. But that innocence, that purity, that emptiness, is bound to be lost because it is unconscious. One has to regain it – one has to gain it consciously. That is the only difference between an ordinary person and the enlightened one.

The ordinary person came with the same potential, has got the same potential still, but he has not claimed it yet. The enlightened one has lost it and claimed it back. The ordinary person is in a state of paradise lost and the enlightened person is in the state of paradise regained. But you can gain it any moment, it is up to you. Nobody can prevent you from becoming enlightened.

It is not a question of any particular talent. Not everybody is a musician and not everybody can be a musician; that is a question of talent. Only a few are musicians and real musicians are born musicians. You can learn the technique; if you go on and on practicing music, sooner or later you will be able to play, but you will still not be a musician. You will only be a technician – one who knows how to play but one who has no inspiration, one who is not really in tune with the music of existence. Music is not flowing through you naturally, spontaneously.

Not everybody can be a poet and not everybody can be a scientist or mathematician; these are talents. But enlightenment is not a question of talents. Everybody is enlightened; to be alive is enough. Life itself is the only need, the only requirement. If you are not dead you can still become enlightened. If you are dead, then of course wait for the next round, but nobody is so dead. People are ninety-nine percent dead, but even if you are one percent alive that is enough. That much fire is enough; it can be kindled, it can be helped. It can be used to create, to trigger more fire in you.

The difference between the enlightened one and the ordinary person is not one of talent. This is the first thing to be remembered, because many people think that it is a question of talent. 'A Jesus is talented, a Buddha is talented; we are not so talented. How can *we* become enlightened?' No, it is not a question of talent at all. You cannot become a Michelangelo and you cannot become a Shakespeare unless you are born one, but you can become a christ, a Buddha.

Everybody is entitled to it, it is everybody's birthright, but you will have to reclaim it. And the effort has to be made consciously. You have lost it simply because you were unconscious. And if you remain unconscious, then the difference will remain. The difference is only of unconsciousness.

Buddha is as ordinary as you are, but he is full of

awareness in his ordinariness. Because of awareness his ordinariness becomes luminous. He lives the same ordinary life, remember it. That is another illusion that people are carrying within themselves: that a Buddha has to be extraordinary, that a Jesus has to walk on water. You cannot walk on water, so how can you be a Jesus? A Buddha has to be special, from the very beginning.

The stories say that before Buddha was born his mother had a few dreams. Those dreams are absolutely necessary. If the mother has not had those dreams before the birth, then the person cannot be a Buddha. Now this is sheer stupidity! Joining Buddha with the dreams of his mother is sheer nonsense, there cannot be a more stupid idea.

And what kind of dreams? Jains have different dreams. Before Mahavira is born, the mother has a few dreams. She sees one white elephant – that is a must. Every *tirthankara*, every prophet of the Jains, before he is born has to be preceded by a dream of the mother of a white elephant – as if the son is going to be a white elephant!

Buddha's mother has to see a few dreams, a series of dreams.... These are just stories, fictitious, created by the followers afterwards. The story is that the mother of a Buddha has to die immediately when he is born, she cannot live. How can she live after such a great phenomenon? It is so vast and so big, the experience is such that it is bigger than death, she simply disappears. Mahavira's mother lives, Jesus' mother lives; they didn't have that idea there – but they have other ideas: that when Jesus is born he has to be born to a virgin mother.

Now people can go to absurdities, to the very extremes of absurdities, just to make one thing settled in your minds: that Jesus is special while you are ordinary. Now where will you find a virgin mother?... you have already missed! Next time maybe you try again to find a virgin mother – and unless you conspire with the Holy Ghost, it is impossible. How will you manage? And then three wise men have to come and a star has to lead them. Now stars don't do that at all, no star can do it. Stars go on their routes; they cannot lead the wise men from the East to the exact place where Jesus is born in a stable, in a poor man's house. Stars can't do that – that is impossible.

These fictitious stories have been invented just to give the idea that you are ordinary and these people are special.

My whole effort here is to proclaim to you that if they are special you are special, if you are ordinary they are ordinary. One thing is certain: you don't belong to different categories, you belong to the same category.

The miracle is not walking on water, the miracle is not walking in fire; the miracle is waking up. That is the real miracle. All else is nonsense.

Wake up... and you are a Buddha! Wake up and you are enlightened! And when you wake up it is not that you will become totally different from your ordinary self; you will be the same person but luminous. You will eat in the same way, but it will not be the same, there will be an intrinsic difference. You will live in the old way, yet it will not be the old because *you* will be new. You will bring a new touch to everything and whatsoever you touch will start turning into gold, will start turning into something meaningful. Before it was meaningless, now it will have significance and meaning. And it is time that you wake up!

The master cannot force you to wake up; the master can only create a situation in which a process can be triggered in you. And *any* situation can be helpful.

Lao Tzu became enlightened just by seeing a leaf, a dry leaf falling from a tree. As the leaf started falling towards the earth, he became enlightened. Now what happened? Seeing the dead leaf falling on the wings of the wind, with no idea of its own, utterly relaxed, utterly surrendered to the winds, he had a glimpse. He must have been in a very vulnerable state. And from that very moment he became a dead leaf in the winds. He surrendered his ego, he surrendered his clinging, he surrendered his own ideas of what should be and should not be. He surrendered all his mind, he simply became a let-go. And that's how he became enlightened.

Anything can trigger the process. Nobody can predict in what moment, in what situation, what is going to trigger the process. It has always happened in such a mysterious way, it is not a scientific phenomenon. It is not a question of cause and effect, otherwise things would have been easier. You heat the water to a hundred degrees and it becomes vapor – but it is not like that. A few people evaporate at zero degrees, a few people evaporate at 100 degrees, a few people evaporate at 1,000 degrees. People are not matter; people are consciousness, people are freedom, so nobody knows what will trigger the process. Not even a master can say that this is going to trigger the process. He can arrange all kinds of devices and he can wait patiently, lovingly, compassionately, prayerfully, and you have to move through all kinds of devices.

Any word may trigger it... or maybe just a pause may trigger it... and suddenly the sleep is gone, the dreams have disappeared. You are born, spiritually born, twice-born. You have again become a child. That's what Buddhahood is, that's what enlightenment is.

Is there really no difference between an ordinary person and one who is enlightened? There is no difference in this sense: that both belong to the same world of consciousness. One is asleep, one is awake; hence the difference. But the difference is only peripheral – not central, not intrinsic, but accidental.

Respect the Buddhas and that will teach you to respect yourself. Respect the Buddhas, but don't condemn yourself. Love yourself because you are also carrying a Buddha within you. You are also carrying a bud, which is going to become a Buddha. Any moment, any day... it can be now, it can be here....

OSHO INTERNATIONAL MEDITATION RESORT

Location: Located 100 miles (160 km) southeast of Mumbai in the thriving modern city of Pune, India, the OSHO International Meditation Resort is a holiday destination with a difference. The Meditation Resort is spread over 40 acres (16 hectares) of spectacular gardens in a gorgeous tree-lined residential area.

Uniqueness: Each year the meditation resort welcomes thousands of people from more than 100 countries. The unique campus provides an opportunity for a direct personal experience of a new way of living – with more awareness, relaxation, celebration and creativity. A great variety of around-the-clock and around-the-year program options are available. Doing nothing and just relaxing is one of them!

All programs are based on the OSHO vision of 'Zorba the Buddha' – a qualitatively new kind of human being who is able *both* to participate creatively in everyday life *and* to relax into silence and meditation.

Meditations: A full daily schedule of meditations for every type of person includes methods that are active and passive, traditional and revolutionary, and in particular the OSHO Active Meditations™. The meditations take place in what must be the world's largest meditation hall, the Osho Auditorium.

Multiversity: Individual sessions, courses and workshops cover everything from creative arts to holistic health, personal transformation, relationship and life transition, work-as-meditation, esoteric sciences, and the 'Zen' approach to sports and recreation. The secret of the Multiversity's success lies in the fact that all its programs are combined with meditation, supporting an understanding that as human beings we are far more than the sum of our parts.

Basho Spa: The luxurious Basho Spa provides for leisurely open-air swimming surrounded by trees and tropical green. The uniquely-styled, spacious Jacuzzi, the saunas, gym, tennis courts … all are enhanced by their stunningly beautiful setting.

Cuisine: A variety of different eating areas serve delicious Western, Asian and Indian vegetarian food – most of it organically grown especially for the meditation resort. Breads and cakes are baked in the resort's own bakery.

Night Life: There are many evening events to choose from – dancing being at the top of the list! Other activities include full-moon meditations beneath the stars, variety shows, music performances and meditations for daily life.

Or you can just enjoy meeting people at the Plaza Café, or walking in the night-time serenity of the gardens of this fairy-tale environment.

Facilities: You can buy all your basic necessities and toiletries in the Galleria. The Multimedia Gallery sells a large range of OSHO media products. There is also a bank, a travel agency and a Cyber Café on-campus. For those who enjoy shopping, Pune provides all options, ranging from traditional and ethnic Indian products to all global brand-name stores.

Accommodation: You can choose to stay in the elegant rooms of the Osho Guesthouse, or for longer stays opt for one of the Living-In program packages. Additionally there is a plentiful variety of nearby hotels and serviced apartments.

www.osho.com/meditationresort